The Marketing

HIGH GROUND

The essential playbook for B2B marketing practitioners everywhere
• *Personas • Positioning • Messaging*

J. Michael Gospe, Jr.
Author of *Marketing Campaign Development*

Foreword by Brian C. Gentile

To product marketers, corporate marketers, and product managers

To advertisers, copywriters, PR managers, and lead generation experts

To marketing practitioners all

Accolades

"The *Marketing High Ground* is an essential read for marketers in the 21st century. Mike reinforces critical marketing fundamentals and provides a concise blueprint for developing customer-oriented business-to-business (B2B) marketing strategies and programs."

Helen Flynn, principal, Flynn Consulting

"Mike Gospe's book is relevant for marketers everywhere. I especially like the way he shows the path to the high ground. And as I'm a visual learner, I found that his examples and illustrations bring the personas and messaging to life!"

Doreen Godfrey, marketing manager, financial services industry

"I'm a big fan of real life case studies, and Mike gives readers the opportunity to see how the concepts are used, especially in the hard to define area of B2B marketing."

Susan Ayoob, publisher relations/marketing, Alcance Media Group

"This is a book on marketing that I can relate to. I was hooked in the first two pages. Mike delivers experienced and practical field-level marketing advice, complete with examples that keep you flipping the pages as compared to other marketing books that drag on and on about the "should do's" and lack the "how to's."

Heather Deem, technology marketer, Candesco Marketing

"Mike Gospe's methodology works! We've been using his persona, positioning statement, and message box techniques to define use cases and go-to-market plans. With his guidance, we're well on our way to the marketing high ground."

John Finch, senior director of product marketing, LiveOps

"I very much enjoyed what Mike has to say. The information is very relevant for us and could be used by our very small team. As none of us are formally trained in marketing, his practical templated approach is something we can handle on our own."

Patricia Guyot, project manager, Kevrenn International

"Gospe writes from the business-to-business marketing trenches. This is a must-read playbook on the topics of personae, positioning statements, and messaging. It serves as an inspiration for marketers everywhere."

DemandGen Report

Acknowledgements

If this book is valuable it is only because I've learned so much from so many marketing experts over the past twenty-five years. Successful marketing in the 21st century will not be attributed to any one, single element. Instead, success reflects an appreciation of a number of marketing best-practice threads woven together in a tapestry that reflects an honest assessment of the customer and the world in which they live.

Thank you to Brian Gentile who opened my eyes to the concept of a marketing high ground. His tutelage prompted me to up-level my marketing game plan, build stronger integrated strategies, and thereby earn my seat at the leadership table. I offer a special thanks to him for penning his thoughts in the Foreword to this book. I could think of no better way to introduce the *Marketing High Ground*.

Thank you to Susan Thomas and Tobey Fitch, two marketing leaders who understand the psychology of buyer behavior. I am indebted to Susan and Tobey for introducing me to the message-box model and allowing me to share the story of how we used it and evolved it together. Upon this framework, I've built variations for creating relevant messaging and use-case scenarios.

People who have generously shared their stories include Ted Ray, Paul Lang, and Craig Brennan. And special thanks to my reviewers: Mary Gospe, Mary Sullivan, Helen Flynn, Doreen Godfrey, Susan Ayoob, Heather Deem, Patricia Guyot, John Finch, the editors at DemandGen Report, and Brian Gentile. Their feedback helped keep me grounded and the material relevant. I also want to thank Joe Bednarski for his fabulous work on the figures and tables shown in this book. My deep thanks also go to the staff at CreateSpace who helped me bring this book to life.

And most importantly, thank you to my many confidants, friends, collaborators, co-conspirators, and leaders who guided me on my own personal journey to the marketing high ground, including: Gerald Markle, Mike Matson, Tom Harms, Monte Smith, Kathy Babcock, Anne Wagner, Scott McNealy, and Brian Gentile.

Foreword

A seat at the table. As marketers, isn't this what we've always wanted? A seat at the leadership table seems straightforward but proves ever elusive, particularly in business-to-business (B2B) high-technology companies. This is because a seat at the table is a privilege, not a right. So, what's a marketer to do? How can we gain the credibility and respect necessary to earn, and then command, this seat? I've always believed that the answers derive from owning the marketing high ground.

Product companies typically begin from humble origins: they build something and they sell it. If the product truly satisfies a new need (or an old need in a new way), then it could sell quite well. And so the functions of engineering and sales lead the way. As long as the company keeps producing improved versions of a successful product and selling it successfully, how can we argue its success? But this approach to market leadership is flawed, because customer needs and wants can shift at any time. Without a "customer advocate" seated at the leadership table as an equal, market opportunities will surely be missed.

Spend enough time in product companies and you'll learn that the vast majority of them are either "engineering-driven" or "sales-driven." In these settings, a seasoned and accomplished marketer becomes frustrated because he's resigned to either pushing a new set of questionably-targeted features or reacting to the "intelligence" gained from the last sales call. Eventually, this model, driven by the engineers and salesmen whose roles and skills were never designed to understand and target complete markets, always runs out of steam. The problem, simply, is that these leaders have put their product on a pedestal or placed it in the center of their universe. From this view, they lose sight of the customer and misunderstand the market.

You can count on one hand those admired technology companies that are "market-driven." *Market-driven* does not mean *marketing-driven*. The answer is not to suggest that a marketing leader should usurp the powers and intellect of her engineering and sales colleagues. Instead, marketing leaders must rise to the role of leading the executive team, and the rest of the organization, to the high ground. No other organizational function is properly suited to do so. So, lead the way we must. As marketers, now more than ever, we own the burden and responsibility to forge this path.

Defining the marketing high ground requires distilling this broad concept into a few phrases. In short form, it represents a deep and constantly-calibrated understanding of both the specific voice of the customer and the broader voices of the market. Importantly, it requires a fact-based understanding of a company's primary market, its ideal customer, and its compelling advantage in the marketplace. Being fact-based is important, but the path to the high ground means more than this. It's easy to conjure anecdotes (just ask any salesperson) and hard-to-assemble facts into real information. Effective product marketers, product managers, and lead generation experts must do more by forming an objective, informed perspective that literally channels the sentiment of the target customer and, therefore, stands beyond reproach. Standing upon the marketing high ground means being the customer's advocate. Only then can company leaders make the best-informed decisions that will guide superior actions in everything they do.

But the marketing high ground is not, and must not be, limited to just the marketing department. Every market-driven company gains its advantage from an incredibly aligned workforce. Such a workforce clearly understands the organization's vision and reason-for-being, its core benefits and the value ascribed to it by customers, and the distinct advantages it possesses over all other alternatives in the marketplace. Ultimately, this is what it means to own the marketing high ground. A marketing team is only as strong and capable as the rest of the organization's understanding of the high ground. Said differently, show me a great marketing company, and I'll show you a company where *every* employee behaves as a marketer.

And so it is now up to you to find and own your path.

In the pages that follow, Mike Gospe has shared key inflection points that have shaped his own personal journey to the marketing high ground. Written as a part memoir, part playbook, he's assembled a powerful and proven set of advice to guide you on your way. You'll learn how to build a representative persona, craft a clear positioning statement that appeals directly to that persona, and weave a powerful story to engage this target customer because the story demonstrates keen understanding of the customer's likely problems, pains, and need for your product. Then, you'll learn to put this newfound insight into motion by socializing the results with all those internally (colleagues, peers, partners) that need to believe and understand the market with the same passion as you. This is the central key to achieving organizational alignment, a superior understanding of the overall market, and a clearer vision of success. The view is simply better from the high ground.

Brian C. Gentile

Contents

Figures & Tables

INTRODUCTION

Marketing takes a day to learn.
Unfortunately it takes a lifetime to master.[1]

Philip Kotler, marketing guru

Marketing. How hard could it be? I mean, really. Sometimes it seems that every engineer, sales rep, and finance manager believes they can do marketing better than someone trained in the field. I used to believe them. They spoke with such ferocity that I must have missed the finer points in my education. So I became subservient to their whims. Like a yo-yo played by a child, I'd spin up and down and out of control, trying to execute seemingly random projects. The department I worked in was never consulted; we were always told. Thank you, Sir. May I have another?

After a few years of running in circles, I forced myself to stop and catch my breath. In a potentially career-limiting move, I asked the dreaded question, "*Why?*" Why was another new data sheet for an existing product needed? Why must an ad appear in the *Wall Street Journal* next Tuesday or we'd lose the sale? Why must we be at a dozen tradeshows when attendance was falling and our competitors were backing out?

Asking why invited conflict and was interpreted as a form of sacrilege. "There's no time for that! I expect it to be done or your next performance evaluation will reflect that you are not a team player!" Ouch.

But, ask I did. Not in a nasty, nasally, whining way, but in a seek-to-better-understand way. In a diplomatic, team-building-consensus way. There were times when I thought they'd show me the door. But a funny thing happened: I started to understand that they didn't always know the reasons why. Action was the cure for not knowing why. Surely, any action was better than none. After all, marketing is easy. Right?

In truth, bad marketing is more abundant than good marketing. Ask any chief marketing officer and he or she will point out an ad or direct-mail piece that belongs in a Hall of

Shame. Bad marketing runs the gamut of inconsistent and ill-timed messaging to confused images that leave the viewers scratching their heads and wondering, if at all, what the advertiser was thinking. In contrast, good marketing is easy to recognize, but much more difficult to do. That's because it's too easy to take shortcuts: Ready, Fire! Fire! Fire! As the pace of business continues to increase, business leaders are driven to meet quarterly or monthly quotas. While this is a de facto standard expected by CEOs and boards of directors, it doesn't always help build relationships and nurture prospects through our sales cycle. In fact, jumping straight to execution without aiming at the right audience with meaningful, relevant messaging at the right time is counterproductive at best, and potentially disastrous to the sales pipeline. In our frenzied approach to collect names and drive leads (any leads!), we've replaced the discipline of thoughtful marketing with hope that a series of quick-to-execute marketing gimmicks will work. That is a dangerous strategy to embrace.

To you, gentle reader, I offer a marketer's call-to-arms: We need to get that discipline back. The job of the marketer is to help sales sell. To do that, we must collectively raise the bar in all that we do, from sensing marketing opportunities, to gathering market requirements, to synthesizing competitive data, to applying customer feedback, to managing the go-to-market plan. Success in today's competitive marketplace requires marketers to take responsibility for understanding the target customer, their pain points, their opportunities, and their buying process better than ever before. Brian Gentile, a consummate marketing professional and alumni to Apple, Sun, and now CEO of Jaspersoft, calls this notion the *marketing high ground*. He defines it as follows:

The Marketing High Ground (noun): that special place where the most capable and competent marketers dwell because they own the never-ending process designed to broadly gather and interpret market-based information on behalf of the company so that superior product/service/go-to-market decisions are always made.[2]

The marketing high ground does not exist in isolation. It is part of a larger operational context that begins with a solid understanding of the corporate strategy and ends with the tactical execution of marketing activities and offers to prospects and customers. Marketers alone cannot claim market leadership for their company. Instead, marketers are the enablers, evangelists, and guides that can rally the entire organization to achieve the greatest success in the marketplace. You can think of this context as having four layers, as illustrated in Figure 1.

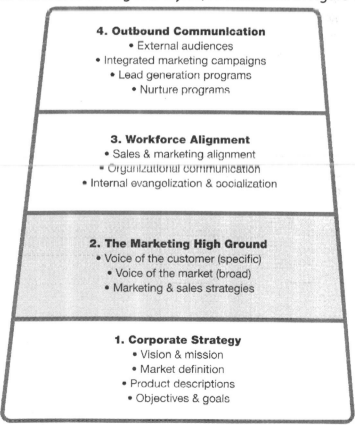

Figure 1: Operational context for the marketing high ground. The focus of this book is on layer 2.

Layer 1: Corporate Strategy. The marketing plan is meaningless if it is not well grounded in the vision and mission for the organization. Market definition, product descriptions, and operational objectives and goals need to set the direction first.

Layer 2: The Marketing High Ground. It is upon the foundational business strategy that the marketing and sales strategies are built. The high ground pays attention to both the *specific* voice of the customer (VOC) and their concerns, worries, problems, and desires in addition to the *broader* voice of the market (VOM) that recognizes insights and ideas that cannot come from customers.

Layer 3: Workforce Alignment. If marketers reach the high ground but fail to *communicate and share* customer insights, perspectives, and behaviors cross-organizationally then they've failed. Marketers must take ownership for aligning marketing with sales and broadly communicating the short-term and longer-term go-to-market strategy. Product roadmap discussions and prioritization of use-case scenarios are captured here. Alignment also ensures that sales and marketing teams work closely together to jointly agree upon a crisp definition of a "qualified lead."

Layer 4: Outbound Communication. Tactical execution follows strategy. Without a marketing high ground foundation that is understood across the organization, marketers can only hope for success. And, hope is not a sustainable marketing plan.

Within the context of these four layers, this book is focused squarely on layer 2: the marketing high ground. My single purpose for this playbook is to help guide you on the path to understanding the customer so well that you become acknowledged as the customers' advocate. The good news is that marketers can greatly improve the results of their campaigns by adopting a few best-practices designed to build a shared understanding of what the customers and prospects value most. Accompanying you on your journey are three critical best practices that will guide your product definitions, go-to-market strategies, and integrated campaigns.

1. ***Building a persona*** *to represent your target market. Personae go beyond traditional market segmentation because they provide an illustration of real people with whom you can empathize.*

2. ***Crafting a positioning statement*** *to focus the differentiating value you offer these personae. A crisp positioning statement is required in order to build a solid messaging framework that will be relevant to customers and prospects.*

3. ***Telling your story*** *using meaningful messages relevant to the needs and desires of your target personae. Today's savvy buyers don't want to be sold to. Instead, they are looking for stories that engage them on elements they care about.*

If you are a product marketer working on the launch of a new product, this book will help you craft the most compelling positioning statements. If you are a product manager, this book will encourage you to tune your use cases and re-evaluate your assumptions about your user personae. And, if you are a demand generation marketer within a large company or a small business, this book will walk you through the steps to develop a winning, integrated, go-to-market strategy. With a renewed sense of empathy for and understanding of the market, you will elevate the marketing department from being just expert tactical trigger-pullers, to also becoming a strategic, valued asset to your business.

For more information on these best practices:

*   Read *Marketing Campaign Development: what marketing executives need to know about architecting global integrated marketing campaigns* (available on Amazon)
*   Visit http://marketinghighground.wordpress.com

Part One: INSPIRATION

What I've learned (so far) on my path to the Marketing High Ground

"Why do you hesitate? He who hesitates is lost."[3]

Gerald Markle, Santa Clara University professor

1

AWAKENING

I wasn't ready. My eyes shifted back and forth, looking alternatively at the chalkboard at the front of the room and my open textbook that dared me to offer an answer. Professor Gerald Markle patiently paced the classroom aisle and stopped in front of my desk. He wore a dark suit with a black tie, casting a gloomy presence that contrasted with the warm spring day that waited outside. When you listened to him, you knew he was smart. The kind of smart that made you think that he had forgotten more than you could ever hope to learn. His index finger gently tapped the small writing block that mimicked a writing surface attached to the institutional chair-desk I sat in. A complex calculus problem required solving at the chalkboard. I slowly raised my gaze and met Markle's. His quick nod confirmed that it was my turn to sink or swim. The class was silent. Proving the formula quickly was required. To pause was an invitation for a lesson in humility.

In 1984, I was a junior at Santa Clara University, working on my BSEE. The windows were open to let in a spring breeze. You might have heard the birds if not for the cars racing down the Alameda, a strip of California's El Camino Real linking Junipero Serra's missions up and down the California countryside. I walked to the board and took a deep breath. The answer was not obvious to me. I did the only thing I could: start with the basic assumptions about the problem in order to solve the riddle. I built a hypothesis based on my assumptions, scribbling on the board to show Markle my thought process. I waited for his "harrumph" that would be a clue that I had made a mistake. Out of the corner of my eye, I saw him standing silently. Observing. Waiting.

"Why do you hesitate? He who hesitates is lost," he said.

My hand was sweating. I almost dropped the chalk. An insight followed my hypothesis. I engaged a formula, made an error but quickly caught it. A minute later, I had an "aha!" moment and I ran for the finish line. I dodged the bullet that day by following a mathematical process with logic and order. As I sat back down, I wondered if real life would ever require me to solve differential equations.

Markle's refrain became a mantra quoted by my friends, often in jest. But I took it to heart in all of my college work. In time, I came to realize that what he really taught me was the importance of knowing a process to solve a riddle and to be quick and confident in my approach. While math equations have a definite precise and correct answer, real life does not. Regardless, Markle's approach was a lesson I learned to apply broadly. Assumptions. Hypothesis. Intuition. Observation. Correction. Solution.

I also started suspecting that becoming an engineer was not my first best destiny.

2

ENGINEER OR MARKETER?

In the spring of 1985 a parade of companies visited campus to interview the year's soon-to-be graduates. Lockheed was *the* company my engineering friends were talking about. Like the clandestine operations found in a Tom Clancy novel, the allure to be part of a secret project was not to be denied. And the annual salary was the highest around at $30,000. They didn't seem to mind that during their first year they'd be sequestered in a building known as the "ice box"—a windowless, institutional high-rise eyesore where they would shuffle papers and do menial tasks, until their security clearances were granted.

I wanted something different. What interested me was the possibility of translating engineering designs and innovations into business language that anyone could understand. And with that decision, I took my first step on the path to becoming a marketer.

Ultimately, I accepted a marketing position at Hewlett-Packard's Microwave Semiconductor Division in San Jose. I became an outcast to many of my college conspirators. "Marketing's not a real job!" they'd laugh. From their perspective, they thought I'd just flushed four years of college down the drain. Yet, I felt exhilarated. Perhaps ironically, I got this job precisely because I was an engineer. Had I graduated with a business degree, I would not have been considered. In Silicon Valley, you're either part of the engineering brotherhood or you're not. And HP was no exception, even in the marketing department.

3

THE LYNCH PIN

My first job was that of a Regional Sales Engineer (RSE), essentially being the lynch pin between the eastern region sales team and the R&D and manufacturing teams at HP's then Microwave Semiconductor Division. I represented sales and their customers' needs to engineers. And vice versa. This job was the only time in my career I would receive training that included shadowing other teammates in their daily role. While my friends were on ice at Lockheed, I spent time in the fabrication labs, worked the assembly lines, partnered with sales, and visited customers. I was a kid in a candy store, learning all I could.

Most people don't realize that making diodes, semiconductors, and transistors is a lot like being a baker. There are recipes to follow. Adding too much salt or using baking soda instead of baking powder can ruin the cake. And as a baker, there is just as much art as science applied to making these electronic components. This became painfully apparent when a sought-after batch of chips could not be reproduced because the recipe had never been written down. Like directions for making Aunt Charlotte's chocolate cake, this recipe was passed around via an oral tradition. Variations were to be expected. But General Dynamics needed 50,000 additional components, precise to the specifications found in the original batch. Alas, the engineers could not readily duplicate the magical mix in large quantities. Although this latest batch might be perfectly good for other applications, slightly out of spec meant they were unusable to GD.

I soon found myself in the middle of heated debates between the sales team believing the engineers were running amok and the engineers believing the sales team was incapable of selling what they had produced. As a newly minted graduate, I was not prepared for internal conflict. I was naïve in thinking that work consisted of like-minded professionals who shared a singular goal and operated as a team. A rude awakening it was.

Yet I was incredibly fortunate to have a role model to guide me. Mike Matson, the marketing department manager, was a polished sales guy with a history of success at Motorola before joining HP. He was personable and levelheaded, with a soft-spoken demeanor. Three divisions made up HP's components group, each having its own marketing manager. But it was Mike who everyone wanted to work for. It took me a while to understand why this was so. To my eyes, he fostered a sense of teamwork and navigated internal politics as easily as Joe Montana won Super Bowls for the San Francisco 49ers.

In those days, the marketing bullpen was nothing more than a collection of desks with a border of non-matching cubicle walls, some yellow, some orange, some brown. Sitting at my desk, I stared at my flickering green 5x7 inch computer screen reading an unending stream of emails about this issue, each growing angrier by the minute. I fretted over how to respond to the growing level of animosity. Emotions had eclipsed logical thought, and there was no shared strategy for helping the customer. I noticed Mike sitting at this desk.

Mike's office included a standard institutional metal desk neatly tucked against a set of windows that overlooked a patch of soon-to-disappear San Jose farmland. He sat silently, as I updated him on the current status. Inside me, I felt the world was near collapse. I did not know what we could promise to lessen the customer's frustration. I could not give sales what they wanted, and I felt frustrated, miserable, and uncertain as to my future at HP.

The exact details of how the situation was ultimately resolved are hazy to me. What I remember most was how Mike played the situation. We proceeded to have a conference call with the regional sales leaders to discuss options. Mike wove a tapestry of diplomacy, balancing leadership and sensitivity. He never once lost his cool, yet he was direct as he addressed the emotional assertions made by the sales team. At the same time, he listened to the concerns of the sales leaders. He took control of the conversation and shifted it from a blame game to a shared action plan. It turned out that there were other concessions that could be offered. He reminded us to return to the values HP was known for, namely caring for the customer in a broader context, valuing the longer-term relationship over today's fire that would burn bright, but only for a short while.

After the call, he explained to me that success would not be defined by a single order but by a long-term partnering relationship with the customer. What I had seen as an isolated black-and-white drama, Mike saw as an opportunity with all the colors of a rainbow. He opened my eyes to see alternatives that could cater to a broader landscape of customer needs.

It was several years later, after having worked for a few hard-to-please or difficult managers, that I realized how lucky I was to have Mike as my first marketing leader. Throughout my career, when I found myself in similar testy circumstances, I would often ask myself, *What would Mike do?* The answer was easy: put the customer, not the product, in the center of the universe, and alternatives can always be found.

4

BUILDING THE BETTER MOUSETRAP

We introduced the "Building a Better Mousetrap" positioning workshop at HP in 1990. I was the press relations manager in the Test & Measurement (T&M) Group working in Santa Clara. Tom Harms, the direct marketing manager, and I were tasked with developing a training program that would help the marketing teams in the T&M divisions do a better job positioning their products. The Mousetrap theme seemed appropriate because most of our marketing colleges were in fact engineers. "Who needs marketing when we build such great products?" they'd exclaim. Who indeed!

So, the concept of our positioning workshop was to confront the often-believed notion offered by Ralph Waldo Emerson: "Build a better mousetrap and the world will beat a path to your door." It's a hard lesson to learn that just because you can build something doesn't mean it will sell. Bravo to the leaders that recognized that the global HP marketing team needed a kick in the butt to elevate its collective skills.

Engineers, in general, are some of the most innovative creative geniuses I'm privileged to know. But they are sometimes myopic, believing that everyone else will see the wisdom and value in anything they create. So, Tom and I, with some humility and a fair amount of coaching from our bosses Monte Smith and Kathy Babcock, took this exercise to heart. We did a lot of research on positioning and messaging by the leading experts. We also read a lot about how to engage our colleagues in facilitated team-based training. Together, we constructed a practical and pragmatic workshop for our motley cross-functional distributed crew. The workshop challenged the team to define the intended audience and avoid the lazy temptation of trying to sell to "everyone." With an unwavering focus on our product, we explored and debated its benefits and features, prioritizing only those benefits that were relevant and meaningful to our target personae. Lastly, we evaluated our work, taking a draconian look at whether we had created something that was truly different from competitive alternatives.

This process of creating a workshop and then learning how to teach it became pivotal in my becoming the marketer I am today. It's one thing to know something and quite another to be able to write it down and teach someone else how to do it. Tom and I gave this workshop at least twenty-five times during my tenure at HP's T&M group. Since that time, I've taken the lessons to heart. Over the next twenty years, I would and still continue to look for ways to improve positioning and messaging best practices.

5

THE STORY OF SUN'S WEBTONE CAMPAIGN

In January of 1997, I worked for Sun as one of its first integrated campaign managers. I remember clearly one of my first leadership team meetings. Anne Wagner, SunSoft's marketing leader relayed to us the gist of the latest executive staff discussion. Scott McNealy, the CEO and founder of Sun, had called his executive team together, and he was not happy. After some careful investigation of the trends driving what would become the dotcom boom, he concluded that seventy-five percent of all servers running the Internet were running the Sun Solaris operating system, and nobody knew it.

Back in 1997, Sun was a hardware box pusher. McNealy saw an opportunity to become something more. He set his sights on Sun becoming the "Internet foundation." What was called for, McNealy explained, was nothing short of repositioning the company. We were tasked to figure out how to make this happen. And we had ninety days.

I panicked. Sun was a product company entrenched in selling boxes. The marketing mechanics, much less the politics involved, would require a Herculean force of will. Then again, McNealy wanted it done. I would learn many lessons over the next two years, not the least of which is the power of having an executive sponsor with a clear vision.

To achieve our objective, we knew we had to break the habits of how Sun traditionally approached marketing. Rather than put the product at the focal point, we realized we needed to understand our target audiences first. Only then would we be able to craft a story that would capture interest and speak to the relevance and opportunity that Internet computing provided. The first questions we chose to address were the following:

1. *Who were our primary target audiences and what did they care about? We needed to understand them.*
2. *How could we help them gain competitive advantage using the Internet more than any competitive alternative? We needed a clear, crisp positioning statement that catered to our target audience.*
3. *What was the most effective way of engaging this target audience in a dialog? We needed a set of clear messaging and a blueprint for engaging them in a conversation over time.*

McNealy challenged us in a way you only read about in a *Harvard Business Review* case study. We were given permission to break rules and start fresh. Although it seemed less than clear at the time, the process of defining the persona, positioning our products to them, and then engaging them in a dialog was groundbreaking. With a newfound respect for the target market, we became energized and empathetic. The result was a wildly successful campaign that produced results for the next two years and helped drive a fourteen percent increase in Sun's annual revenue.[4, 5]

6

GUERILLA MARKETING AND THE DOTCOM BOOM

I wanted to take the marketing practices I had learned from giants like HP and Sun and apply them to smaller companies and start-ups. Yet, I had trouble applying these process-heavy best practices. Because smaller companies don't have the staff and resources of their big brothers, I required a more nimble approach to integrated marketing. It was during these years that I learned what it really meant to sacrifice. Working as an executive with a small company, I alone was responsible for managing our small budget. It became painfully obvious how little marketing muscle we could afford. We required focus and prioritization. There was just no way to successfully market to multiple market segments with our limited staff and budget. We had no choice but to be strict and to get serious about what Jay Levinson calls "Guerilla Marketing."

I was the VP of marketing for an innovative, knowledge-management start-up at the time when Google was just starting out. Addressing the frustration of customers being placed on hold when calling for customer support, our company built one of the first Web-based, virtual call-center agents. Customers could interact with a "virtual agent," ask their questions, and get real answers without ever needing to pick up the phone. Our customers saved tens of thousands of dollars per month in call-center operations by making it possible for customers to find answers to their most common questions online, instead of via the phone.

We were young and bold, so we decided to aim for CEOs of big companies that generated thousands of customer support inquiries every day. These companies would be ideal showcases for our product and technology. We could have purchased a list of names of a thousand executives from a thousand companies and blanketed these unsuspecting souls with email, direct mail, and telemarketing. But we didn't. Instead, we chose to build our own smaller list of a hundred companies we felt would appreciate our product. Our plan was to engage each CEO in a dialog, one at a time. However, to win a meeting with them, we knew we couldn't just tell our story; we had to show our story. And to do that, we needed two things: the CEO's email address and a relevant business problem they were experiencing that we could help solve. We researched each company and looked at how they were engaging in customer support, both via phone and via the Web. Our hook was to empathize with their challenges and to illustrate a new venue for directing a portion of their customer traffic. This would be accomplished with a picture, literally, of what our Web-based support interface, branded as their own, might look like on their website.

Putting these emails together was labor intensive. We had no money, so guerrilla marketing was our only option. To do this, we deputized our professional services team to mock up a screen shot of our product, branded to each individual company on our target list, complete with their logo, color scheme, and then we added content relevant to their products and services. Just one look communicated the power of what this customer support interface could do for them. It also had a "cool" factor.

To manage the process, we made a schedule to produce and distribute ten custom emails every week. I wrote the email on behalf of our CEO. It was a simple paragraph that introduced himself as a fellow CEO with a crazy idea that might help the target CEO with a customer-support problem or opportunity. Included was the mocked-up screen shot. The call to action was personal: "Let me know if you think this is a crazy idea." The email was not longer than twenty lines. No list of features, no jargon, no sales language or marketing fluff.

Over six weeks, we achieved an unheard of thirty percent response rate. We received responses from the CEOs of UPS, FedEx, AT&T, and a variety of others. My favorite came from Michael Eisner, then head of Disney. He wrote a personal note and included the names and contact information of his two customer-support VPs, asking them to meet with us! Not only were doors opened, the red carpet was rolled out. Just think what we might have achieved had we had money!

Walking the path to the marketing high ground does not require a large staff or a sizeable budget. It only requires that marketers understand the target customers. This marketing campaign worked because we took the time to understand the target customer, connect with them on an issue they worried about, and then initiate a relevant, meaningful dialog with them on their terms.

7

MARKETING LESSONS FOR THE 21st CENTURY

After twenty-five years of perpetual motion in a variety of roles in marketing, I've learned that what once was old is now new. The dotcom boom came, and there were voices adamant that the old rules of marketing no longer applied. They were wrong. Today, the excitement and hype around social media is tempting some people in the same way, with some marketers leaning towards over-investing in social media at the expense of a balanced, integrated marketing plan.

The best advice I can give marketers is to always remember that successful marketing is not about technology, marketing automation, social media, or whatever breakthrough comes next. It's about understanding the target customer, what makes them tick, what information they are looking for, and how they wish to collect and consume that information.

There is a discipline that must be applied to gathering this knowledge and sharing it internally, so that superior product, services, and go-to-market decisions are always made. Otherwise, key pieces of customer knowledge and perspective remain locked in people's heads where they are fragmented, undocumented, and hidden from view. The path to the marketing high ground begins with four critical exercises:

1. *Zeroing in on the bull's eye in a target market segment*
2. *Illustrating a targeted audience (persona) that lives in this segment*
3. *Designing a crisp positioning statement relevant to the persona*
4. *Crafting a set of relevant messages that engages the persona*

I learned through trial and error that when I embraced these steps my marketing campaigns succeeded. When I took shortcuts or skipped even one of these steps, the results were less satisfactory. I thought I was saving time, but instead, I wasted money and lost time.

The best practices illustrated in this playbook are time tested and proven to work. I don't care if you are promoting hardware, software, or services. Success is always directly tied to how well you know your audience. Use these best practices. Adopt them and make them your own. They will serve you well. In the pages that follow I will show you how.

Part Two: INFLUENCE

How to design and critique a powerful positioning statement

"Great communicators have an appreciation for positioning. They understand the people they're trying to reach and what they can and can't hear. They send their message in through an open door rather than trying to push it through a wall." [6]

John Kotter, Harvard Business School

8

DOES YOUR COMPANY HAVE A POSITIONING CRISIS?

When it comes to "positioning," just about every marketer says they do it and that they are comfortable with their results. And, to be sure, there are a lot of seasoned pros that know from practical experience what this exercise is truly about. Yet, for the rest of us, the art and science of product or corporate positioning is still a bit of a mystery. How do you know if your organization has a shared understanding of the central value your product provides customers? An easy test is to ask a few of your executives and peers, separately, "What is our positioning statement?" It's not unusual to get different answers, sometimes wildly different answers. This, gentle reader, is a huge red flag. The red flag may be a result of a *poorly crafted* positioning statement, or a *poorly communicated* one. Together, we'll explore how to solve both of these problems.

Without a common framework and an agreement on the words to use, people in your organization will have differing understandings of your product's value. Sales, service, marketing, and engineering teams will not be aligned. The result: miss-directed sales reps, ineffective marketing campaigns, and avoidable conflicts between marketing and engineering regarding the product roadmap. How can you avoid these miss-understandings? During these turbulent economic times, coupled with the rapid evolution of technology, the most seasoned marketers review their positioning strategy once or twice a year. Table 1 reveals a few clues that your product positioning may need some attention.

CLUES THAT YOUR POSITIONING STATEMENT SHOULD BE REVISITED:

Change of agency: The marketing team has changed advertising agencies more than once in the past year because "they don't understand our business."

Change of strategy: Your company has recently changed its strategy, but the rank and file have not been informed of the details. In the meantime, the team continues to execute the status quo marketing campaigns.

Frustration: Marketing managers are frustrated that their writers "just don't get it!" There are too many rewrites. It takes the marketing/PR team more than three drafts to finalize a press release, direct mail piece, or data sheet.

Rambling sales reps: It takes the average sales rep more than 30 seconds to describe the product and its value.

Never done: Oops, we've never documented our marketing strategy or positioning statement.

No single source: Each sales rep has a different "elevator pitch."

Out of alignment: The VP of Marketing and VP of Sales have conflicting perspectives on the positioning and sales tactics. There is no common definition of a "lead". The Sales team is writing its own collateral, opting not to use marketing-created sales tools.

Out of date: It's been a year since the executive team reviewed the positioning strategy.

Table 1: Does your company share any of these symptoms? If so, your positioning statement may be in need of review.

9

WHAT IS A POSITIONING STATEMENT?

When I ask marketers to *show* me the "positioning statement" they've crafted, I get a wide variety of illustrations. It's not uncommon for a marketing communications manager to boldly recite their slogan—five or ten words spoken with conviction and energy. On occasion, I've had product-marketing managers and sales reps hand me a multi-page document that recites their company's history. "Read this!" they say with annoyance, as if the positioning should be obvious to me. In other cases, I've been lectured by product managers about their technology or handed a twenty-page document with many tables, graphics, and notes scribbled in the margin. Sometimes marketers believe their data sheet is the positioning statement; in other cases, it's a (very long) Microsoft PowerPoint™ presentation used by sales. And most often, it's not a statement at all. Instead, the positioning thought is buried deep within a lengthy marketing plan, with positioning statement elements scattered across the pages, putting the burden on the reader to make sense of it all.

While each of these examples (tagline, company history, technical whitepaper, presentations) is an important deliverable along the continuum of a product's lifecycle, none of them is a true statement of the product's position in the marketplace. The tagline is a string of words designed to be memorable, while conveying a brand promise with emotion. It is an *output* or a result of having a good positioning statement. The same goes for customer-viewable presentations and whitepapers. The numerous tables, charts, scribbles-in-the-margin documents are best thought of as *inputs* that will guide the development of a positioning statement. Crafting a well-thought-out positioning statement takes time; it's a process of discovery. It's easy to capture notes, opinions, facts, and figures. Instead of prioritizing and making hard choices to hone the product's go-to-market strategy, we jam-pack every bit of detail into a corporate presentation and expect the prospective customer to sort out what is really important. This only confuses customers and unnecessarily lengthens the sales cycle.

Instead, marketers need a template to help them distill all this important information down into a crisp, tightly focused positioning statement that everyone in the organization can understand with clarity and conviction.

So, by definition . . .

The **positioning statement** is a subset of a value proposition that optimizes it for marketing communications purposes. It identifies the target audience, the product and its category, a specific benefit, and is differentiable from the nearest competitive alternative. It is an *internal, non-emotional statement* that becomes the messaging cornerstone of an integrated marketing campaign.

There is often confusion between value propositions and positioning statements. While they are often used interchangeably, it is important to understand the differences. Value propositions encapsulate a summation of benefits offered to multiple market segments and the price for those benefits. Positioning statements, in turn, represent a plea for single-mindedness and an opportunity to be focused on one audience at a time while exercising only a relevant differentiable benefit. Multiple positioning statements may be encompassed by a broader value proposition. Value propositions are not covered in this book; however, value proposition templates and examples can be found in my book, *Marketing Campaign Development: what marketing executives need to know about architecting global integrated marketing campaigns* (available on Amazon.com). *Marketing Campaign Development* shines the light on constructing and executing global integrated marketing campaigns and includes a variety of templates, illustrations, and examples.

In the pages that follow, we'll explore the elements of crafting and communicating an effective positioning statement and how and why this is crucial to a marketer's success.

_____ 10_____

WHY POSITIONING STATEMENTS ARE CRITICAL FOR SUCCESS

Do we really need a positioning statement? Absolutely. Here are three true stories that illustrate the value of a good positioning statement and the tragedy that can result from not having one.

1. Why the lack of a positioning statement cost a start-up its financing

A luminary and well-respected leader was invited to attend a critical board meeting of a Silicon Valley start-up company. The executive team had feverishly worked to invent and position the company, and this meeting was their one chance to gain a critical endorsement that would lead to more and better financing options. With introductions completed, the CEO and VP of engineering began to relay the genesis of the start-up with passion and detail. Fifteen minutes later, the luminary politely raised his hand and asked them to stop. He said, "I still don't get what you do." The silence was palpable.

What went wrong? There was no "Aha!" moment as they described the business problem they addressed and the compelling benefits they offered. The CEO and VP of engineering were under the illusion that their credentials, plus a passion for their technology, would be enough to win favor. Instead, their audience had no patience for the technical details. The luminary wanted to know the following:

- *Who was the target audience(s)? How big was the target segment?*
- *What problems or opportunities did they face?*
- *How were these people addressing these issues today?*
- *What was the differentiating value this new product offered these potential customers?*
- *To sum it all up: why should these prospects care?*

Instead of delivering a business plan based firmly on a crisp, focused positioning statement, they delivered a rambling monologue where the upshot for the business was less than obvious. Unfortunately for these company executives, the luminary was not impressed. The opportunity to clearly articulate the relevance of their new product had been missed. There would be no second chance.

2. How the positioning statement saved a company's reputation

One of my personal "Aha!" moments about the importance of having a clear product positioning statement came about during my tenure as a press relations manager with HP's Test & Measurement group (prior to HP's spinoff that would become Agilent). One of the divisions had just developed a next-generation signal generator and was eager to introduce it. The engineering team quickly drafted a press release with the following headline:

HP Introduces High-performance Signal Generator with New Low Price

Upon first glance, this seemed like a perfectly reasonable headline. Yet, my "spider-sense" tingles when I see primary benefits linked to pricing. I wanted to be doubly sure that I understood exactly what this meant. So, I pulled the engineering team together to talk about their draft.

Their first reaction was something like, "Oh great, you're one of those guys" —meaning that I was an outsider with the sole purpose of upsetting their applecart by asking a lot of nonsense questions. With great diplomacy, I admitted that it was my job to work with them in order to confirm and communicate the product's truest value related to the claims they were making.

I asked if they had produced a positioning statement for the product.

They handed me a five-page, feature-rich datasheet that only confused me. Not to be put off, I suggested we take thirty minutes to build a positioning statement for the product. I explained that this would help us confirm the primary benefit and focus our message.

In the course of our discussion, we filled out the positioning statement template (see Chapter 11), and learned a few key things, especially when we dug into the primary benefit and the differentiator:

1. *This new signal generator was actually more expensive than competitive alternatives! However...*
2. *This one box could perform multiple tests without the need for additional pieces of expensive equipment.*
3. *The upshot: this was really a total cost of ownership (TCO) story, not a component box story.*

With newfound clarity we wrote a new headline based on this positioning statement:

HP's New High-performance Signal Generator Reduces Test Costs

So what? Did this exercise really matter? You bet! Had we proceeded with the original headline, editors (not to mention customers) would have quickly cried "foul!" HP's reputation would have been hurt by the misleading claim made in the original headline. Instead, this clarified positioning statement wove its way through the press release, print advertising, collateral, and other customer pieces. Following the product announcement, articles appearing in technical journals echoed the positioning statement correctly and completely. As a result, this product found huge success with new and current customers alike. And all it took was thirty minutes!

3. *How positioning statements save time and money (and reduce frustration!)*

A true warning sign that there are problems with a product's positioning lies in the number of iterations it takes to write copy. Early in my career, when I worked for HP and Sun, it was not unusual for a press release to require as many as nine revisions before it was finished. Nine! Similarly, direct-mail pieces, product brochures, and data sheets could take many months to write and get approved, all because the messaging was in flux due to a poorly contrived positioning strategy.

Message flux is a sign of weak positioning. It's weak in the sense that the team hasn't completely thought through the implications, or that there remains some significant differences of opinion.

During my tenure at Sun, I was a campaign manager for one of the business units. The press relations manager working on a launch with me was continually at odds with the product marketing team, because the team kept changing the emphasis for the press release. She and I would sit in her office and try to decipher why we were having so much trouble articulating the product strategy and drafting the release. In times of duress, she would use aromatherapy to try to clear her head. The occasional Friday afternoon might find her sequestered in her office with only the flickering light of an Ocean Rain-scented candle or the effervescent smell of a Hawaiian White Ginger potpourri to transport her to a less stressful place. I'd visit with her during her mental holidays and we'd share a laugh, trying to put our frustration into some perspective.

It was during one of these conversations that we took a hard look at the process we were following with the cross-functional team—a process that mainly consisted of adhering to "he who yelled the loudest." We both knew that this was not an effective way to direct a product launch, yet we were uncertain about how we could influence a change of behavior.

One thing was clear: there was no positioning statement acting as a rudder for the launch. This particular launch had already cost too much time and effort, and we decided that the best approach was to let it run its political course. However, we also decided that we would approach things differently for the next launch.

In so doing, we introduced a template for a positioning statement (see Chapter 11). She and I spent time with the product marketing director to develop a focused picture of the target buyer, their concerns and business drivers, our primary benefits, and our unique differentiation. The result: the exercise of drafting a clean, fill-in-the-blanks template generated a constructive dialog that kept us on track. To our surprise and delight, others in the organization were waiting for someone to guide a structured conversation, as opposed to the agenda-less, freeform meetings of the past.

With the introduction of the positioning statement template, and the process of facilitating the discussion to complete it, it became much easier to discover and resolve differences of opinion. And, each time a new launch or product release was scheduled, the positioning statement exercise was part of the process. It became easier to do each time. And it became much easier to gain approval before any effort was put forth to write copy. On average, press releases now required only three iterations, and each one was limited to small edits and not major rewrites. In addition, accompanying direct mail pieces and collateral were produced in a matter of a couple of weeks instead of months. Yes, it saved money and time. More importantly, it saved our sanity and produced a tighter bond with the cross-functional team.

11

INTRODUCING THE POSITIONING STATEMENT

Positioning statements come in all formats and lengths; however, I've found the template in Figure 2 to be the most helpful and succinct. The definition of the positioning statement is further illustrated in Table 2. The theory behind this tool comes from Jack Trout and Al Ries, the authors of *Positioning: The Battle for Your Mind.*

To: _____
(Target Persona)

_____ **is the one**
(Product Name)

_____ **that**
(Category)

_____ **unlike**
(Key Customer Benefit)

_____
(Nearest Competitive Alternative)

Figure 2: This positioning statement template has all the appearances of being a simple fill-in-the-blanks formula, but don't be deceived. It's trickier than it first appears.[7]

The purpose of the positioning statement is to align marketers, product managers, and sales representatives so they act more effectively as an integrated team with a shared view of the market. Success requires that everyone in the organization understands and embraces this core value statement. Failure to be aligned will yield a muddled interpretation of the marketing strategy and a set of messages that are irrelevant, off target, and confusing to prospects and customers.

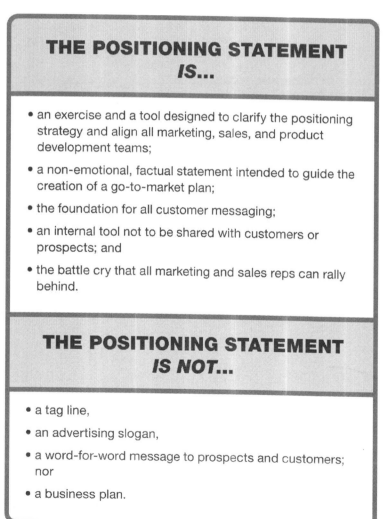

THE POSITIONING STATEMENT IS...

- an exercise and a tool designed to clarify the positioning strategy and align all marketing, sales, and product development teams;
- a non-emotional, factual statement intended to guide the creation of a go-to-market plan;
- the foundation for all customer messaging;
- an internal tool not to be shared with customers or prospects; and
- the battle cry that all marketing and sales reps can rally behind.

THE POSITIONING STATEMENT IS NOT...

- a tag line,
- an advertising slogan,
- a word-for-word message to prospects and customers; nor
- a business plan.

Table 2: Further definition of the positioning statement.

Before we dissect this template, a bit of perspective is in order. What does a good positioning statement look like? Indeed, there is a lot of confusion about "good" versus "not so good" versus "confusing" and "just plain wrong." To understand the difference, consider the observation that positioning statements tend to fall into one of three types: 1) all benefits, 2) favorable points of difference, and 3) just what the customer values.[8]

All benefits: The most common positioning statements are really no more than a long laundry list of features disguised as benefits. The more, the better, right? Wrong. The problem is that features do not equal benefits. And, customers don't really care about every benefit. There is so much information contained in this type of positioning statement that the key points are drowned out by the surrounding noise. While this level of positioning is insufficient, it does represent a good start from which we can build.

Favorable points of difference: Other marketers go further by considering that the customer always has an alternative. They pay attention to differentiators against all competitors. Unfortunately, they often make the mistake of assuming that any and every favorable point of difference is important and must therefore also be communicated to every customer, whether it's relevant or not. They err on the side of being complete, not realizing that they have over-complicated the positioning statement. And, of course, saying that the solution is better than competitor X's is only relevant if the customer is viewing competitor X's solution as an alternative.

Just what the customer values: Best-practice marketers hone their positioning statements on only those few elements that matter most to target customers, focusing on the clear, differentiated value relevant to that particular market segment. They are able to credibly demonstrate the superiority of their offering, as compared against the nearest competitive alternative, and communicate it in a way that conveys a sophisticated understanding of the target segment's concerns, issues, and business priorities.

With a clear definition of the positioning statement, let's now examine each line element, starting with the target audience.

12

LINE 1: TARGET SEGMENTATION
AND THE PERSONA

The bull's eye and persona exercises are the most effective (and fun) ways to ensure team alignment regarding the prioritization of the target audience.

A shortcut to traditional market segmentation

Target market segmentation is an essential part of planning. Yet, traditional market segmentation brings to mind an academic, time-consuming, and costly process. If you are fortunate enough to have the time, money, and resources to conduct an in-depth segmentation analysis using focus groups and primary and secondary research, then go for it! However, most of us probably don't have that luxury. We need to begin executing our strategy on Tuesday. So, what can we do?

Fortunately, there is a shortcut that allows marketers to build and test a *segmentation hypothesis* that we can start working against. Building the hypothesis starts when marketers look within their own company to find peers, colleagues, and co-workers who have valuable, relevant insight and perspectives regarding customers and why they buy. Where are these people? They reside in sales, marketing, product management, and customer support. Hidden inside their collective heads are the perspectives about the problems the customers are trying to solve and the criteria they use when making purchase decisions. Unfortunately, corporate memory is short and often undocumented. But, when marketing leaders step up to capture, structure, and document assumptions about customers and prospects, they discover they have enough information to form a segmentation hypothesis and prioritize target segments. Capturing and documenting these assumptions starts with the bull's eye exercise.

Identifying the bull's eye

The first step in prioritizing segments is to be mindful of the trap of "trying to be all things to all people." We are victims of our own desire to sell to anyone and everyone. Collectively speaking, in our race to help sales make quarterly numbers, marketing teams fall into the trap of casting as wide a net as possible for fear of leaving out a potential audience segment. Unfortunately, this approach of broad inclusiveness leads to a mish-mash of messages and an unfocused marketing campaign that actually extends the sales cycle because it takes longer for customers to understand our offering. Instead, we stand a much greater chance of success if we can laser focus our messages to become relevant to a prioritized set of potential buyers. In this way, the task of market segmentation is like aiming for the bull's eye: the sweet spot consisting of those key folks most likely to buy the product now.

Start by asking product leaders to define the target market. If you get an answer like, "We want chief information officers (CIOs) of the global 5000," then we need to raise a yellow flag. There are several problems with a segmentation description like this.

1. *The "global 5000" represents the largest 5000 companies, based on annual revenue. This is much too broad a statement to be helpful, because it assumes that each of these companies thinks and*

behaves the same way. We know this is not true. The global 5000 may include a range of companies that earn between $10 million and $100 billion, or have between one hundred and one hundred thousand employees. It's easy to see that revenue or employee base alone varies wildly here. These variations will cascade through operations, financial planning, and buying processes. In short, this is no different from saying our target audience is "everyone."

2. **There is no indication in this statement as to the business, operational, or financial problems that these companies are facing.** Where is the opportunity with this segment? Where is the compelling reason to them to buy our product? A good segmentation description makes this readily apparent.

3. **Lastly, companies don't make purchase decisions; people do.** While the statement does indicate that our target is CIOs, it begs the question about why. Traditionally, using job titles makes sense because we can buy lists based on job titles. But job titles are fluid. We need to layer that with a description of key responsibilities because, while job titles may vary from company to company, key responsibilities are more consistent. For example, someone is responsible for a company's IT infrastructure, whether they are titled CIO, IT director, or office manager. Three different titles; same responsibility. Focus on the responsibility first, the title second.

The *who, where,* and *why* of the bull's eye

As part of our shortcut, when it comes to prioritizing and honing in on a target market segment, there are three dimensions to consider, as illustrated in Figure 3. The perfect target segment for us includes those individuals that reflect *all three dimensions* illustrated in bull's eye graphic.

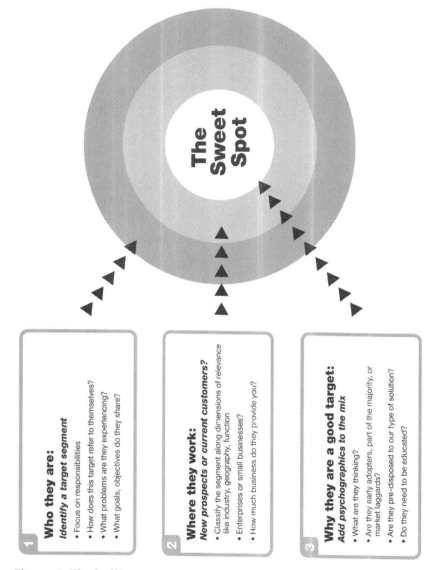

Who they are:
Identify a target segment
- Focus on responsibilities
- How does this target refer to themselves?
- What problems are they experiencing?
- What goals, objectives do they share?

Where they work:
New prospects or current customers?
- Classify the segment along dimensions of relevance like industry, geography, function
- Enterprises or small businesses?
- How much business do they provide you?

Why they are a good target:
Add psychographics to the mix
- What are they thinking?
- Are they early adopters, part of the majority, or market laggards?
- Are they pre-disposed to our type of solution?
- Do they need to be educated?

Figure 3: The bull's eye template is an excellent way to prioritize and focus in on a segment sweet spot.

Figure 4 offers an example of the bull's eye technique used by marketers selling wireless access products and services.

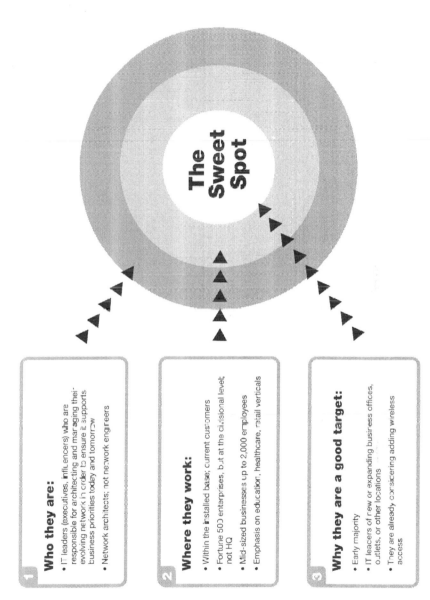

The Sweet Spot

Who they are:
- IT leaders (executives, influencers) who are responsible for architecting and managing their evolving network in order to ensure it supports business priorities today and tomorrow
- Network architects; not network engineers

Where they work:
- Within the installed base; current customers
- Fortune 500 enterprises, but at the divisional level; not HQ
- Mid-sized businesses up to 2,000 employees
- Emphasis on education, healthcare, retail verticals

Why they are a good target:
- Early majority
- IT leaders of new or expanding business offices, outlets, or other locations
- They are already considering adding wireless access

Figure 4: Example of a bull's eye segmentation description developed by a marketing team within a large technology company.

Who? As previously discussed, we need a description of a specific individual (or group of individuals) within a type of company or organization. Identifying responsibilities, in addition to applicable titles, is an excellent way to start. The example illustrated in Figure 4 was the output of a segmentation discussion I conducted with a marketing team in a large technology company. When I asked them to define their target segment, they said "everyone." We then drilled down to focus on "CIOs." But this still was too broad. In the course of our conversation, we asked sales reps to describe the last sale they had made, who bought the product, and why they won the business. This was very telling: in the three case studies that sales shared with the team, each sale was made by a different titled individual: a CIO, a network architect, a technology specialist. *While each title was different, the key area of responsibility was the same*: they were responsible for designing and managing their evolving network. With that in mind, we honed in on this responsibility and created a list of possible job titles that are typically mapped to owning this responsibility. This became our outer circle.

Where? Imagine double-clicking on the outer circle. What would be the *next layer* of details? Addressing the *Where?* layer is the next logical dimension. Specifically, do these prospects know who we are? Are they currently customers of ours? Or do they not know us? This is where we also consider company sizes, geography, and their history. This is represented in the middle layer. Let's return to the example in Figure 4. The team debated the priority for mining the installed base (current customers) versus finding a brand new set of potential customers. What ultimately tipped the scales was the urgency of driving the sales pipeline. For sales to hit their quarterly numbers, new opportunities needed to be discovered within days and weeks. It would take too long to find and nurture new prospects. It is a truism that it is easier to sell to current customers than to new customers, so the team decided to prioritize its efforts and target a segment that already knew the company, its products, and its values. However, just leaving the inner circle as "installed base" was far too broad. After all, the installed base represented many customers of all sizes and shapes. Some additional details were required. Large enterprises were prioritized; small-to-medium-sized businesses were excluded. And finally, a prioritization of industry segments was added. When taken together, the combination of the outer and middle circles begins to paint a picture of an ideal target segment *demographic,* complete with key descriptors, dimensions, and areas of responsibility. But still, one key piece is missing.

Why?Why do these individuals represent an ideal segment? To answer this, we need to know a bit about how they think. We need to know their *psychographics*. What predispositions do they have as to why they make purchase decisions? Are they early adopters or laggards? What are their preferences? Are they already aware of solution alternatives, or do they need to be educated? Where are they in their buying process? Let's return once more to the illustration in Figure 4. In this case, the marketing and sales teams felt strongly that it would be easier to sell to individuals who were already considering wireless technology solutions. Those potential customers did not need to be educated on why adding this new technology made sense. They'd already crossed that bridge. In fact, they were likely already involved in evaluating competitive solutions. What's more, the application of the new technology could be sold equally well to "green field" environments (e.g., a brand new building or an expanding company where new office space was being added). In short, the easiest target to sell to were the folks who already knew what they were looking for, understood the benefits, and were already evaluating options. The inner circle represents the likely responsiveness the target segment may have, based on its psychographics, behaviors, and the timing of its buying cycle.

The upshot of the bull's eye exercise is that it forces marketers to hone their understanding of potential target segments in order to decide which ones to *proactively* address. "Proactive" is the key word here. Failure to proactively prioritize target segments leads to *reactive* marketing, where hope is the central ingredient, as in, "I hope this *tactic du jour* will work." But hope is not a marketing strategy. The expected results of a reactive plan will have you wondering which half of the budget is ill spent. You won't know, because the marketing programs and messages are ad hoc and random, yielding inconsistent results. The ability to achieve optimum marketing return on investment (ROI) requires sacrificing the desire to lasso multiple, unrelated audiences at the same time. Do so at your own peril, because you'll end up watering down the message to its most generic form. Instead, set your sights on the bull's eye and don't wait for them to come to you.

Illustrating the persona

While rationalizing and prioritizing a target market segment is a good start, it is not sufficient to guarantee that we truly understand the people who will hopefully buy our products. We need a persona for each type of target buyer. Building a persona is about understanding the prospective buyer; it's about walking in their shoes to better feel, taste, touch, and smell the trends and priorities that shape their purchase behavior. If we fail to empathize with the buyer, then we increase the risk that our messages will be ignored. We'll fail to connect.

A **persona** is a personalized extension of the bull's eye exercise. It is a detailed fictional representation of a targeted buyer represented by demographics and psychographics found in one or more classes of real people. While a persona isn't a real person, he or she must feel like a real person.

2-3 Word Description of the Persona

Who they are:

		Photo to illustrate the persona
Name/Gender/Age	Give your persona a name; make them human	
Education	Describe their background	
Title / Responsibility	Job titles vary from company to company so also focus on the key responsibilities	
Role in the Purchase	Decision maker, influencer, purchaser, advisor, analyst, user, or other?	
Attitude	Attitudes can say a lot about how they view their job, role, problems, and opportunities. They also provide clues to the language you can use to connect with them	
Reputation	How are they viewed inside the company?	

Where they work:

Ideal company profile	Include relevant dimensions like company size, industry, familiarity with your products and services, how much business they do with your company, et cetera

Why they are a good target (for your product):

Values	When making a purchase decision, what's important to them? Consider dimensions like leadership, innovation, knowledge and expertise, return-on-investment, saving money, improved productivity, things that make their job easier, or things that make them successful
Fear	What keeps this person up at night? What are they afraid of? Consider negative outcomes such as project failure, getting fired, cost overruns, or even peer pressure
Pet Peeves	What do they hate about the products, how they are used, their own purchase cycle, or the vendors' sales cycle?
Information sources	Where do they get their information? Who do they turn to when they have questions? Google? Peers? Vendors' websites? Analysts?

Figure 5: This is a generic persona template. Include only information relevant for the product or service being promoted.

By looking at the product from the persona's point of view, we can better understand the buyer. And as such, a clearer communications strategy will result because:

- *Messages can be focused on topics that are most relevant to the target buyer.*
- *Superfluous information and over-specifications can be eliminated.*
- *Features can be prioritized according to the persona's values.*

In practical terms, a persona can be illustrated in a one-page template, commonly captured in a slide or table, as shown in Figure 5. Distilled from dozens of documents, plan drafts, and other sources of corporate knowledge, this single page serves a key purpose: to produce a clean, crisp picture of the targeted buyer that can be easily shared internally. This tool is essential for aligning marketing and sales teams. Imagine if everyone in marketing and sales had the same illustration hanging on their cubicle walls, the same uniform understanding of the buyers and their business priorities, goals, and buying tendencies. Creating a verbose marketing plan with lots of details is easy. But that weighty tome is difficult to share broadly internally in hopes of ensuring that everyone reads it and interprets the data correctly. Distilling it down to a simple illustration is more digestible.

While illustrations of personae will vary widely from company to company, a simple template provides a good starting point. Keep in mind that the final persona illustration will be shaped by dimensions that are relevant to your own unique business. A persona for a CIO in a hi-tech company will contain different elements from a persona for a hospital administrator; a persona for a small business telecom manager will convey insights very different from a persona used to illustrate supply-chain managers at major retailers. Regardless, all persona exercises begin by asking marketing teams questions about the buyer's demographics, psychographics, priorities, and business drivers. The template shown in Figure 5 offers only a generic starting point. Here are a couple of examples of real personae created by marketing teams and executive leaders I've worked with.

- *"The Globetrotter"[9]—a frequent flyer business executive, represented in Figure 6.*
- *"The Conflicted Procrastinator"[10]—a call center director, represented in Figure 7.*
- *The "Corporate Radical"[11]—a senior executive at companies producing more than five thousand customer comments/feedback per month, represented in Figure 8.*

There are a couple of things to notice across these examples:

1. *Each persona has a story to tell, capturing relevant points (demographics, psychographics, priorities, and business drivers).* *The marketer must empathize with the persona in order to make a connection. Give the persona a name and a face. This makes empathizing with them much easier.*
2. *While the three personae are similar, the template has some noticeable differences.* *The template is meant to be a guide—not a straightjacket. If some information doesn't fit, don't include it. Want to add an additional element? If it is relevant, go ahead! Make the template fit your business.*
3. *To summarize the exercise, find one, two, or three words that best describe your persona: "Globetrotter," "Conflicted Procrastinator," and "Corporate Radical."* *This becomes your shorthand label for your persona. Write this label in the "persona" blank in the positioning statement.*

The globetrotter: frequent flyer business executive

Who they are:

Name/Gender/Age	John K.; 40 – 55 (50/50 male/female)
Education	Post graduate; earns >$150K/year
Title / Responsibility	CXO, sales leaders, or other business leaders who manage outsourced or overseas operations; Sales leaders who are always travelling, especially internationally
Role in the Purchase	Decision maker (when it comes to personal health or productivity issues that arise while travelling/conducting business)
Attitude	Has a positive "can do" attitude; solutions-focused; positive and up-beat
Reputation	A "road warrior"; highly regarded; a frequent flyer recognized by their airline(s) of choice

Where they work:

Ideal company profile	Silicon Valley hi-tech companies who have outsourced operations overseas, and/or that have sales or other executives who travel more than two weeks per month or 100,000 miles per year

Why they are a good target for a jetlag remedy:

Values	High personal-productivity while on the road; Doing business via face-to-face meetings with employees and customers
Fear	Travel fatigue that impacts their ability to conduct business; losing time or business opportunities because they did not arrive at their destination with a 100% energy level
Pet Peeves	Ineffective or unhealthy stimulants; getting sick while travelling
Information sources	Work peers, executive forums, or other frequent flyers, (Airline) frequent flyer newsletters, and in-flight promotions

Figure 6: The "Globetrotter" persona hones in on travel-related concerns and priorities. Notice the implied differences between him and the occasional, non-business traveler.

The conflicted procrastinator: the uncertain call center leader

Who they are:

Name/Gender/Age	Robert B., 35 - 45 (50/50 male/female)
Education	College degree; prior role: supervisor of routing/analytics
Title / Responsibility	Responsible for meeting service-level agreements and minimizing costs
Role in the Purchase	Drive the team responsible for considering upgrades and new technologies required to evolve the call center. He's a gatekeeper and an influencer
Attitude	Skeptical, frugal, a procrastinator – keeping the status quo is a safer bet because a failed implementation will cost him his bonus. Big ego. "Likes to be shmoozed."
Reputation	Risk averse. He's also a job hopper with no allegiance to the company

Where they work:

Ideal company profile	Major enterprises (HQ or divisional) with the following characteristics: maturing business, federated model, multivendor technology IT environment. They have multiple call centers more than seventy five seats and are staffed with their own agents

Why they are a good target for an on-demand contact center solution:

Values	**Team Leadership:** Sees the big picture; knows a lot about customers, products, company culture **Knowledge & Expertise:** Studies call center trends and collects knowledge; is technology savvy **Innovation:** A laggard. Requires proof points on how others have successfully applied new technologies
Fear	Making a bad purchase decision that detracts from his compensation and advancement opportunities
Pet Peeves	Self-serving vendors who don't understand his business; implementation woes
Information sources	Peers/colleagues, Google search, Call Center associations, vendors, analysts

Figure 7: The "Conflicted Procrastinator" reflects the attitude of a call center director who is reluctant to upgrade his equipment for fear of making a bad purchase decision. He is deliberate, slow to making a decision, and requires proof.

The corporate radical: the executive "change agent"

Who they are:

Name/Gender/Age	Charlene E., 40 – 50 years (50/50 male/female)
Education	BS plus MBA
Title / Responsibility	VP of Marketing or VP of Products which includes responsibility for leading an internal initiative to make better decisions based on customer feedback
Role in the Purchase	Decision maker. Members of her team will evaluate technologies and solutions to help her organization build stronger affinity with customers
Attitude	Leader; business savvy; high energy; passionate
Reputation	Visionary; decisive; well-regarded in the organization. She has worked her way up the organizational ladder

Where they work:

Ideal company profile	Customer-facing global enterprise companies that generate more than 5,000 pieces of customer comments/feedback per month (via phone, letter, email, social media). Prioritized industry segments include: telecommunications, Internet retail, consumer

Why they are a good target for an on-demand customer feedback solution:

Values	**Leadership:** works hard to promote positive change that adds value. **Highly customer-centric:** seen as the customer's advocate. **Early adopter:** personally interested in social media and the latest trends of customer interaction
Fear	Waiting too long or failing to act quickly to meet customers' evolving needs and expectations
Pet Peeves	Slow-moving vendors and employees who don't share her passion
Information sources	Peers/colleagues across marketing, customer support, call center communities, Google search, white papers, case studies

Figure 8: The "Corporate Radical" is directed at executives who yearn to be agents of change in their company.

How many personae do you need?

This is a good question. The answer depends on how many separate markets you want to address, and how many different types of people are involved in the buying process. Remember earlier in this chapter when we introduced the CIO, network architect, and technologist? We were looking at job titles relevant to the *Who?* circle of the bull's eye example. In that particular case, we would only require a single persona, not three. This is because we can choose to focus on the one responsibility that is shared, not the three different job titles.

Let's keep things in perspective. If you are a small company with a single product, chances are your best efforts will be achieved by focusing on one or a manageable few market segments. If the targeted buyer is similar across these few segments, then you can get away with a single persona. If, on the other hand, you are part of a marketing team at a large technology company that caters to many markets across the world, you will likely need multiple personae. Yet, these personae may share points in common—like cousins. So, perhaps you'll end up with a parent persona with several variations that are determined by geography or experience (e.g., CIOs of start-ups in developing nations may have different priorities and tendencies than CIOs in mid-sized US businesses). You'll discover the right answer as you start to illustrate your personae.

In either case, don't overdo it. Keep things simple. While you may have multiple audiences to cater to, prioritize them based on which ones are easiest to sell to. Nail those first. Even as you focus on a niche, be aware that others will hear your message, too. There will be a halo effect, as non-intended audiences respond to your marketing efforts. Of course, you will gladly accept their money, but don't get distracted. Keep the focus on the persona that resides in the bull's eye.

What about non-profits?

Personae apply equally well any time a company wants to encourage an audience to take a specific course of action. In marketing and sales, the goal is to get the prospect to buy. In the non-profit world, the goal may be to get people to donate money, volunteer, engage community members, or even vote a certain way. It doesn't matter; the persona exercise and template works in the same way. In order to entice people to take the action we want them to take, we need to understand them. Again, it's all about using this as a tool to illustrate our segments so we can empathize with them and ultimately engage them on their terms, on topics that matter to them.

What about the complex sales process?

It's true that there can be many people engaged in a complex sales process: influencers, decision makers, recommenders, users, and buyers. In an academic sense, they need their own persona. But I like to keep things simple. If we can carefully and correctly identify the primary persona (usually the decision maker), then others surrounding the persona will benefit from our marketing messages, offers, and activities, as well.

Practically speaking, it would be a laborious exercise to create personae for every touch point in the sales process. Yet that may be what is required. My recommendation is to start small. Build a persona for the decision maker first, then construct an integrated marketing campaign to provide the content, information, and messages he requires. Design marketing tools and collateral with the expectation that it can and will be shared with others in the prospect's organization. For information on how to engage prospects and nurture them through their buying cycle, please refer to *Marketing Campaign Development: what executives need to know about architecting global integrated marketing campaigns*, available on Amazon.com.

A final word about the persona

Is this exercise really necessary?

You bet. A case in point: After guiding a marketing team through this exercise, they socialized the resulting persona with the VP and regional sales leaders. Two of the most telling pieces of feedback were:

"Historically, we've been selling too low into the organization. We need to aim higher, and this is the right target for us."

"I've been selling to this group for five years and I've never seen the persona written down before. You got it right. This is exactly who I'm meeting with this afternoon."

Talk about a confidence boost to the marketing team.

As I've said before, there is not enough time, money, or energy to be all things to all people. Successful marketing requires focus. And it requires sacrifice. And, yes, deciding to prioritize and focus on a sub-segment is risky. After all, what if you guess wrong? However, think about it this way: If you guess correctly, then your marketing ROI is guaranteed to be greatly improved. If you do guess wrong, then you quickly find out what not to do and you can move on to the next segment with confidence. Either way, you win by avoiding wasting precious time and money and unnecessarily lengthening the sales cycle.

13

LINES 2 & 3: NAMES AND CATEGORIES

Now that we've covered the target persona in Line 1, we can move on to the product and category of Lines 2 and 3. How you view your product may not be how the customer views it. Perceptions are reality. And your reality must align with the perceptions of the targeted persona. Your positioning strategy must be tuned accordingly.

What's in a name?

The name is the tag or label that the consumer uses to order or purchase the product or service. The name can be as simple as an identifier or even a part number, like the Swingline Model 67 Electric Stapler. Or it can be as robust as a brand name, having a unique and identifiable personality, like Microsoft Windows™.

The brand is a powerful corporate asset. Customers have long rewarded companies by supporting products with known and trusted names. A customer who trusts a brand name will seek it out, pay a premium for it, resist offers from others to switch, and possibly experiment with product-line extensions that carry the brand's name. Branding can be done at just about any level in a company. Some companies brand the company name as well as their product lines, like Sony and Intel ("It's a Sony," "Intel Inside"). Other companies, such as Proctor & Gamble, invest heavily in product brands (Tide, Jiff). Branding can add great value to a corporation, product, or service and is therefore an intrinsic aspect of a marketing strategy.

While all products do need a name, each product does not require its own brand. For example, Hewlett-Packard has a reputation for delivering quality and highly reliable computers, printers, and technology products and services. Since 1939, customers have associated these attributes with HP because they found that HP consistently met or exceeded the expected performance requirements. Over time, the value of the HP name began to mean something. As a naming convention, HP uses a strategy that promotes the corporate HP brand first, the product line name second, such as with the HP Photosmart C4780 All-in-One Printer. This is not just a matter of company pride or a routine labeling convention. It's a reflection of the equity inherent in the HP name. So, if the intended image of the product or service is consistent with the overall image of the company, branding at the product or service level may be unnecessary.

However, should a company wish to promote a different set of attributes than those already associated with the company or product or service line, an alternate image may be required. Thus, the second decision in a branding strategy is to determine what "image" you want for your brand.

Image means personality. Products and services, like people, have personalities. The personality of a product or service is an amalgam of many things—its name, its packaging, its price, the style of its advertising, and, above all, the nature of the product or service itself. But, if the consumer's beliefs and experiences with the product or service are at variance with the promoted attributes, you may be in trouble. As authors

Al Ries and Jack Trout will tell you, marketing is often more a battle of perceptions than of products or services.[12]

So, how do you want your customers to identify your product or service? What name do you want associated with it? And how is it listed on your price list? This name is what you should write in the "Name" blank in the positioning statement.

Identifying the category

Whereas the product or service name is factual, perhaps bland, and obvious, the "category" offers an invitation for creativity. The category refers to the group, family, type, or kind of thing in which the product or service belongs.

Some years ago, I heard the story of the Porsche 911. During the dotcom boom, life was good for car dealers, and especially good to a local Porsche dealership in the San Francisco Bay Area. Whereas other marketing and sales teams would be content to ride the gravy train as long as it lasted, the leadership team at the Porsche dealership wanted to know exactly why business was so good. They decided to engage in a small bit of primary research. After the paperwork was signed, as they were handing over the keys, they asked each customer a simple, open-ended question: *"If you hadn't purchased the Porsche 911, what would you have bought instead?"*

Now, all auto dealerships were experiencing a spike in sales during this period. As such, the marketers felt certain that the customers would answer with competing brands: a Jaguar, a Lexus, a BMW. But that's not at all what they heard. After several weeks of asking this single, straightforward question to several dozen new customers, the top two answers were:

1. *A down-payment on a second home*
2. *A European vacation*

So, in what category does the Porsche 911 belong? Here's a hint: it's not an automobile!

The category can be cut and dried: *the Porsche 911 is a car*. Or, it can be bold and imaginative: *the Porsche 911 is a luxury item*. How you decide to categorize your product or service will have a profound affect on how you market it. The intangible attributes of the category will influence your messages and provoke an emotional reaction from customers and prospects.

If you were Porsche's director of marketing, consider how this newly found data might reshape your target market segmentation and personae. Instead of pushing product comparisons against other cars, you might consider promoting the 911 as a status symbol that nestles right up against the Rolex watches, spa treatments, and first class air travel. For the executive who's made it to the top and wants to make a personal statement of success, this is the car for you!

Cracking the category

You can capture a strong position by creating a new category and naming yourself number one. After all, there is no point in launching a new product or service in a new category, unless you can be first in that category. With that in mind, the first question to ask yourself is "First what?" The search for a unique product or service category offers the opportunity for creative thought. Table 3 illustrates a sampling of companies, products, or services that were able to capture a leadership position by creating and promoting a new category in which to compete.

Categories offer marketers the opportunity to think outside of the box. In 1992, marketers at RCA launched an ad campaign with the headline: "The RCA 35" Home Theatre. So real, it's scary."[13] This was the first time that I ever saw the words "home" and "theatre" used in the same sentence. While each of the words (home, theatre) was certainly common, the new two-word phrase offered a new thought and a promise of a new experience. A new category was born.

GENERIC CATEGORY	NEW CATEGORY
When is a television not a **television**?	When it's a **home theater** (e.g. RCA big screen TVs)
When is an MP3 player not an **MP3 player**?	When it's a **personal digital media player** (e.g. Apple iPod)
When is a truck not a **truck**?	When it's a **sports utility vehicle** (e.g. Toyota 4Runner)
When is a candy not just a **candy**?	When it's an **after dinner mint** (e.g. After Eight Thin Mints)
When is a shipping and packaging business not just a **shipping and packaging business**?	When it's your **personal branch office** (e.g. FedEx with the acquisition of Kinkos)

Table 3: Creativity with categories

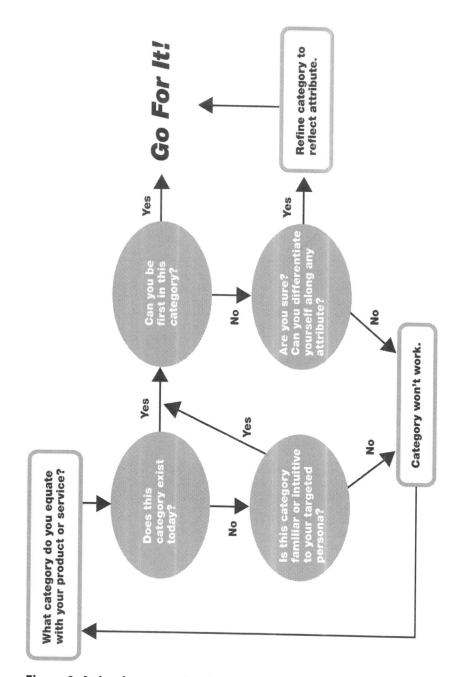

Figure 9: A simple process for determining a new category

There are many different ways to be first. When you are first in a new category, promote the category. But, what's the process for determining a category that works for your product or service?

Potential categories are limited only by your imagination. Figure 9 illustrates a simple process for vetting potential categories. A good product or service category is understandable, even if it is new to customers. Customers can visualize "home theater" or "personal branch office" even though those words may never have been combined in the same sentence before. Focus on those product or service attributes that help distinguish or differentiate your product or service. The category that results from this process is what you should write in the "Category" blank in the positioning statement.

Matching products and services to categories via the reference ladder

Once you have determined the name for your product or service and the category that you wish to promote it in, you have one last test to pass: the test of matching the product or service to the category. It's not enough to choose a name and a category in isolation of each other. This match must make sense, be intuitive, and reasonable to the customer. If he or she isn't sure of what you are talking about, you've lost your chance to capture customer interest.

**Reference Ladder
of Cars Known
for Safety**

Volvo

Toyota

Dodge Chrysler

Buick

Figure 10: The Reference Ladder. How would you rank these cars based on safety? Who's at the top, and who's at the bottom?

All products and services are not valued equally. There's a hierarchy that prospects use to evaluate and rank alternative products. We can visualize this hierarchy as a product or service ladder in the customer's mind, with each rung having the name of a product or service. The best products are more highly ranked and earn a position at the top of the ladder. Take the automobile industry, focusing on the safety niche, as illustrated in Figure 10. If I ask you, "Which car brand is best known for safety?" You'd likely say Volvo, and that answer would be largely acknowledged as true. But, if I suggested Toyota (circa 2010) is best known for safety, many people might be Incredulous. In 2010, Toyota suffered a string of quality issues that put the safety of their cars into question. So, who's on the top rung of the auto safety ladder and who's not?

The mind is selective, deciding which product attributes and benefits are important and relevant. People use their ladders every day in deciding which information to accept or reject. Only data that is compatible and consistent with its product or service ladder in that category will be accepted. Otherwise, it will be ignored. Build your own reference ladders based on your own personal experience. What does your reference ladder look like: who's on top and who's on the bottom? Table 4 offers some fun examples. I offer these examples in hopes that you may take issue with the rankings. This is exactly the point of the reference ladder exercise. If and when disagreements arise, it is critical for the marketer to understand why. It's not about conveying truth; it's about understanding perception.

Imagine your proposed category as a ladder in the prospect's mind. Your goal is to gain a recognizable and defensible position on this ladder, with higher being better, but there is always an exception: remember the Hertz versus Avis story? Hertz is the number one car rental service in the US; Avis is the second largest. Avis didn't want to fight for the top position directly. Instead, they created a strategy around being #2. The "we try harder" tagline has been working for Avis for years. Regardless of your position on the ladder, the ladder must be upright. By that, I mean that the category the ladder represents must make sense to prospects and customers.

CATEGORY EXAMPLES

	TV Commercials	Department Stores	Cars	Fabrics	Books
High class	American Express	Nordstrom's	Porsche	Silk	Classics
Medium class	Bank of America	Macy's	Lexus	Wool	Best sellers
Low class	Geico Insurance	Target	Ford	80/20 Poly-cotton	Romances
No class	Eastwood Insurance	Kmart	Yugo	Polyester	Comic books

Table 4: Reference ladder examples

In every case, it is imperative that you have a realistic view of where your product or service sits on the ladder. Which competitors are above you and which are below you? Don't create a category based on jargon. Remember to speak the consumer's language, as your product or service and its category must fit into your customer's frame of reference. Customer and prospects must be able to compare your product or service to other solutions that solve the same problem. If they don't or can't understand the value that you bring and differentiate it against competitive alternatives, your message will miss the mark.

14

LINE 4: REACHING THE PROSPECT WITH A GOOD KEY BENEFIT

A common mistake made by many marketers is confusing features and benefits. When developing a positioning statement, one of the key ingredients is in identifying the most compelling benefit relevant to the target audience or persona. Features are related to product attributes: it comes in blue; it's round; it prints thirty pages per minute. True benefits answer the "so what?" question. Benefit statements may be about saving time, improving productivity, or achieving higher levels of measureable success.

Marketers occasionally fall into the trap of believing "more is better." It's not. They are reluctant to limit the number of benefits their product offers for fear of missing a key element the prospect cares about. The irony is that people are overloaded with messages every day. We only push people away when we load up the benefit plate, thereby requiring the prospect to sort through the mess in order to find those benefits that are important to them. This is also a sign that, perhaps, you don't understand the target buyer enough. It is up to the marketer to determine what key benefit, or subset of benefits, are relevant to each prospect, and when and how to present them.

Remember, not all benefits are meaningful and relevant. We need a way to sift through the distractions to find what the prospect values most. To do that, here are five criteria that will help you articulate a good, meaningful benefit. Failure to meet any of these criteria should challenge you to rethink your positioning options. To illustrate each point, let's play off of the mousetrap theme. We want to catch a mouse. The benefit is what we might use to bait the trap.

1) Is the benefit singular and specific?

What is the best bait to use in our basic snap-trap mousetrap? If we're not sure, we might try to bait it with a variety of tasty treats in hopes that one will attract the mouse. We might offer a piece of bread, an egg, a piece of fruit, and a sampling of cheeses. After all, more is better, right? The mouse is stupid and will go for something, surely! We just need him to engage ever so briefly, and then WHACK . . . he is ours! Unfortunately, when we try to cram all of these enticements together, they don't all fit on the trigger platform. Not to be put off, we force them to fit, ending up with a mashed collection of confused benefits that is just not appetizing.

TIP: Be focused on a single benefit (or a small collection of benefits that fit logically together). When marketers try to include a data sheet full of features disguised as benefits, they confuse the marketplace and look foolish.

2) Is it relevant?

We could offer money to mice, but that would just be silly. Intuitively, we know that mice don't care about dollars and cents. Yet, everyone is interested in money, so this seems like it might be a safe bet—especially if we aren't totally sure what the mouse truly values. After all, maybe there is value in a wadded up dollar bill that the mouse could use as part of his nest. Perhaps nesting materials are more important than food. More likely, the real confusion may be in not being able to separate the benefits we understand from the benefits the prospects care about. We need to ask the question, "so what?" Why would the prospect care about this benefit? And, is this benefit more meaningful and relevant than others we might provide?

TIP: Just because a benefit is true to you (the manufacturer), it may not be relevant to the target audience. Ask "so what?" and challenge your assumptions.

3) Is it sustainable?

How fresh are the benefits we are offering? Let's say we offer cheese to our mouse, but that the cheese expired in 2010. Hmm, stale cheese or fresh cheese? Intuitively, we know which one is the better option. I once worked on the introduction of a new oscilloscope with the key benefit in the speed it could take scientific readings. No other scope on the market could work as fast as this. Faster readings in nano-seconds meant more accurate testing could be accomplished in less time. The company spent a lot of money on an integrated marketing program to promote this singular and differentiating benefit. To our dismay, the day before our very public launch, our competitor ran an ad for their new oscilloscope. Unfortunately, theirs ran just a bit faster than ours! While the benefit was singular and specific, and very relevant, it was not sustainable. It was only of value until a competitor out-performed us.

TIP: Is this something you can claim for very long? A benefit related to speed and productivity is only valid until the competition does it faster.

4) Is it believable?

If we offered Velveeta to mice with a sign that said "real cheese," would this benefit be believable? Surely not to the cheese aficionado with impeccable taste, something I suspect of our gentle targeted mouse.

Marketing is a creative art, and today's most effective marketing campaigns are the ones that engage prospects in storytelling. To that end, one could argue that believability is actually more important than the actual truth. Sure, PT Barnum said there's a sucker born every minute. But marketers need to be better than weaving hyperbole. As a legal and ethical matter, marketers must convey the truth without overstatement or exaggeration, lest our company's reputation and relationship with customers and prospects suffer greatly. So, we must offer benefits that are consistent to our brand promise, our history, and within a range of logical possibility.

TIP: Will the target audience laugh at your benefit or shrug it off in disbelief? Will they believe your company's ability to deliver the benefit? How does this compare against current perceptions about your company?

5) Can we substantiate the benefit?

If we offer a hunk of orange cheese and claim it's 100 percent real cheese, is this a good benefit? It is if we can prove it. This is where the power of endorsements and evidence enter the mix. Evidence is what makes you credible in the eyes of customers and prospects. It is the undisputable facts that establish credibility by offering substantiation that your message is accurate and true. Evidence may take the form of customer testimonials, benchmark studies, analyst's reviews, third-party product comparisons, and analysis.

But watch out! In our rush to market, we sometimes take short cuts that result in common evidence mistakes such as those listed in Table 5.

COMMON EVIDENCE MISTAKES

Comparing us to us

Citing our opinions as evidence

Presenting rankings that compare unfavorably to previous rankings

Using sources that are not credible to the customer

Relying on competitive feature comparisons alone

Using old data sources or lifetime averages instead of current data

Citing evidence that does not support key messages

Failing to use or acknowledge the original sources

Table 5: Common evidence mistakes can ruin credibility.[14]

The best place to start in your search for evidence is not "What evidence is available?" Instead, we should ask, "What evidence is needed to make the strongest, most credible positioning statement?" To that end, we may need to do some homework to collect the required evidence. Once you decide on what proof points you need, you can develop an action plan to generate it. Let me be clear, I am not talking about manufacturing evidence. I am talking about taking action in order to collect the evidence that is required. Actions may include interviewing customers, arranging for third-party product comparisons, talking with analysts, conducting focus groups, monitoring online forums, or updating benchmark studies. What's at stake here is nothing short of a company's ethics and moral standing. Customers and prospects can tell the difference and will act accordingly.

TIP: Avoid producing marketing hype. Make sure you have data and evidence to support any claims you make.

_____15_____

LINE 5: COMPETITIVE DIFFERENTIATION—WHY SHOULD I BUY FROM YOU?

Has this ever happened to you?

A product manager summons the team to articulate a differentiator that is distinctive and unique. A list of features and benefits is created, and a debate follows regarding which elements are the most important and relevant. After some discussion, a competitive differentiator is sketched on the whiteboard. You read the result and know that *your top competitor could say the exact same thing!* Looking around the room, you see the team is frustrated and exhausted. Rather than point out the obvious "me too" implication of this suggested differentiator, you decide to go with the flow and leave the discussion for another day.

Determining and articulating a product's differentiation can be a challenge to many marketers. The pace of product development continues to increase, while product lifespans are shrinking. This means that product commoditization shortens the window for establishing and maintaining a recognized point of differentiation. And when products become commoditized, no matter what its history, the default and remaining differentiator will always be price. Unfortunately, prices can easily be beat (at the cost of profitability), making holding on to that point of competitive differentiation tenuous.

What does product differentiation really mean? It means looking at the differences between products, how they are used, and the experiences they provide the buyer or user. Differentiation looks to make a product more attractive by contrasting its unique qualities with other competing products. Successful product differentiation creates a competitive advantage for the seller, as customers view these products as unique or superior. However, all points of differentiation are not equal. Referring back to the three types of positioning statements described in Chapter 11, a good differentiator must reflect similar thinking. It must be:

- ***Relevant to the target persona***
- ***Applicable to the nearest competitive alternative***

Ford may highlight its differentiator as being "made in the USA" to offset the appeal from foreign alternatives. However, if the customer is interested in the safest family sedan around, they'll probably be thinking about a Volvo. The manufactured location may be a true point of differentiation, but if the customer doesn't care about it in the final analysis, it's meaningless.

The good news for marketers is that differentiation can be achieved through many means: feature set, unique messaging, quality of service and support, product reliability, availability through sales channels, packaging, environmental impact, and customer experiences. You are only limited by your creativity. But where do you start? Sifting through a seemingly endless list of possible differentiators can be overwhelming. Here's a technique to help you sort it all out.

Firsts, bests, and onlys

In developing and launching a new product (or even supporting an old product), there are three primary audiences that should be included in the final evaluation of the positioning statement and the salient points of competitive differentiation: internal leaders, external experts, and customers. Surveying each of these audiences, even if done informally, can yield some surprising and helpful results. What we're looking for are the "firsts, bests, and onlys."

- *Were we first to market? Which features or benefits can we claim to be first in providing?*
- *What do we do better than the competition? Which features and benefits can we claim to be the best at delivering?*
- *What is truly unique about our solution? What aspects of our solution can we claim to be the only provider of?*

Interviewing internal leaders

Everyone has an opinion. Let's face it: some matter more than others. In any case, every opportunity to socialize, review, and further focus the positioning statement is time well spent. Having said that, sometimes these meetings can be unhelpful if they aren't structured. One way to guide these discussions is by using an agenda such as the following:

1. *Ask the internal leader/expert to summarize the product offering in non-technical jargon.*
2. *What business, operational, technical, or personal problem does the product alleviate?*
3. *What's really new?*
4. *So what? Why does this matter?*
5. *Of the top ten features and benefits, which ones are truly firsts, bests and onlys?*

When I worked at Sun, I frequently needed to get input and background from "distinguished engineers"(DE)—the most brilliant, decorated technology leaders in the company.

When I first arrived at Sun, I didn't know how to approach these individuals, and frankly, I was a bit intimidated. I often became stuck in their offices for many hours as they gave me a history lesson in subjects that were outside of my realm of interest or understanding. Not wanting to be rude, I was locked in these meetings without a way to get back to the subject at hand. That's when I adopted the structured agenda approach based on these five questions. To my relief, the valuable content immediately bubbled up to the surface, and these meetings often could be shortened to thirty minutes. The DEs also appreciated my direct approach. They'd rather be coding or tinkering anyway.

Testing with external experts

Companies can be well served by testing their positioning statements with external experts: analysts, editors, and unbiased third parties. These audiences share some healthy skepticism and can guide you on the relevance of competitive comparisons—but only to a degree. They know the industry better than they know your product. So, you'll have to illustrate your points of differentiation via use cases, technological evaluations, or other proof points. Better yet, engage these experts by asking them to perform their own comparisons and tell you what they found. This approach takes time. However, if your company has a healthy, constructive relationship with research analysts like the Gartners or IDCs of the world, why not build time into your development cycle for them to play with your product. Yes, there is a risk that their findings won't favor your product. However, it's better to find that out earlier rather than later.

Listening to the customer

The only opinion that really matters, however, is the customer's. So, find a way to ask them why they bought your product. Some sales teams incorporate a win/loss analysis as the final step in their standard sales process, noting these key details in their customer relationship management (CRM) system. Many other teams may have this information, but it's locked in the heads of their sales reps where it's never written down or shared with marketing. But my sense is that most marketers have no clue as to why the customer purchased from them. This needs to be fixed.

The ideal solution is to automate the collection of this data within a CRM system that both marketing and sales can refer to often and with confidence. That can be costly and time consuming; I won't deny that. But it's well worth the investment, as it's a critical tool for helping you reach the marketing high ground. Today's world class companies got that way, in no small part, because they have learned to listen to their customers to better understand what makes them tick.

Don't worry. You don't have to tackle the entire project all at once. Instead, start with a shortcut—a way to start building your own *"voice of the customer"* (VOC) program. This will help you refine your positioning statement and validate points of competitive differentiation. Chapter 16 offers a sidebar on building such a program.

_____16_____

A SIDEBAR ON "VOICE OF THE CUSTOMER" PROGRAMS

This process of discovery builds knowledge that can be shared internally, and it goes a long way toward defining a clear picture about the segmentation priorities that can be tested. Over time, this knowledge base grows. And when this process is incorporated into the marketing team's DNA, prioritizing and defending segmentation decisions becomes much easier. The easiest way to capture this distributed insight is to interview teammates, collect notes, and create a *directory of customer information* that everyone can access and update.

As a way to get started, one company created a simple "Customer Trip Report" template. Every time a marketer visited a customer, they'd write down insights about the customer's use case, pain points, challenges, et cetera. After a while of collecting this data, trends began to immerge from these reports. Intranets, internal wikis, Microsoft SharePoint™, even a shared hard drive offer a good place to post shared customer content. One company I worked with took the extra step to set up an *online war room*, complete with easily sortable tips for the sales team, tidbits on competitive happenings, and videos on how to give the corporate pitch. Depending on your creativity and network infrastructure you can create a more sophisticated repository of "voice of the customer" (VOC) data. This is the era of social media. It's much easier now to have everyone contribute and participate.

A comprehensive VOC program is represented in Figure 11. Each of the three layers has a unique purpose for gathering specific types of information.

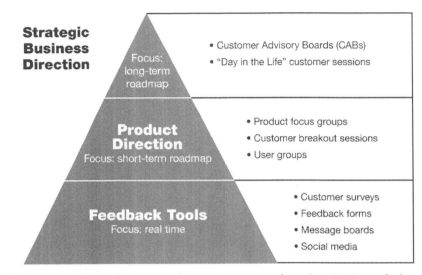

Strategic Business Direction

Focus: long-term roadmap
- Customer Advisory Boards (CABs)
- "Day in the Life" customer sessions

Product Direction
Focus: short-term roadmap
- Product focus groups
- Customer breakout sessions
- User groups

Feedback Tools
Focus: real time
- Customer surveys
- Feedback forms
- Message boards
- Social media

Figure 11: Three layers make up a comprehensive "voice of the customer" program.

Starting at the bottom of the pyramid and working upwards, the first layer reflects the use of feedback tools: surveys, feedback forms, message boards, or social media. After a customer purchases a product, email her a simple survey asking her why she bought from you. If and when possible, have a five-minute conversation with the buyer to ask her a few questions. Find out whom she compared you against. Online survey tools like SurveyMonkey.com are free. Others may have a small fee. These tools are easy to set up and use, cost little money, and can quickly provide you some insight. There are also best-practice techniques for creating online and in-person surveys that are not covered in this book, but I will share two rules of thumb to guide you: 1) keep the survey short and simple, and 2) ask focused questions that will guide you to make appropriate decisions and take action.

If you ask questions that provide vague answers and aren't helpful in understanding why the customer bought, then you either asked the wrong question or stated the question incorrectly.

For a more comprehensive approach to gathering and monitoring customer feedback across multiple channels, including social media, emails, text messages, voice-to-text comments, web forms, and surveys, check out a company called Overtone (www.overtone.com). They make listening to customers a lot easier. Their OpenMic™ product not only enables companies to gather all sorts of customer feedback, it provides alerts and processes data leading to the discovery of hot issues, trends, and patterns.

The middle layer provides an opportunity for more in depth discussion and analysis via focus groups or user group meetings. The purpose here is to explore product directions. These types of sessions typically allow for dialog with and between a small group of customers. Usually multiple focus groups, conducted in various locations around the country or the world, are conducted as part of a larger program. These focus groups are usually most productive when facilitated by an unbiased outsider. They may be conducted blind, where the attendees don't know what company is asking the questions; or they may be company hosted. Focus groups are quite common and can produce some keen insight. The most productive focus groups I've participated in are the ones centered around customer user cases, starting with a description of the a customer problem, issue or an illustration of what the customer is trying to accomplish. In other words, don't start with feature X and ask the customer "what do you think of feature X?" Instead, set the context first. There will be plenty of time to talk about feature X. Hearing customers explain what they are doing and comparing and contrasting product alternatives, in their own words, can be eye opening.

And finally, the top of the pyramid offers a venue to explore strategic directions with senior customer executives who are responsible for planning their company's future. Whereas product focus groups engage users and managers, a Customer Advisory Board (CAB) is a business-level focus group with senior executives. A typical CAB agenda will include topics such as trends shaping the customers' businesses, to business priorities, to shared company-customer initiatives. The CAB is also a productive sounding board for your CEO and executive team to test ideas and preview business plans with leaders from your most strategic customers. This representative group of customers (ideally eight to twelve) meets once or twice during the year. Usually facilitated, these meetings are a great way to validate your company's vision, ensuring that the product direction is in sync with your customers' business plans and priorities.

In contrast, a "Day in the Life" customer session is a type of market research program aimed at understanding one customer at a time. While I worked at HP, we conducted such a program. My team represented HP's service and support business, and we wanted to understand how we could provide better value to our target audiences, namely CIOs, IT managers, and administrators. We visited a dozen companies where we facilitated a dialog with their IT team (with the help of an outside consultant) to better understand everything they did in a course of any given day. Questions we asked included things like: *What's the first thing you do when an employee logs a helpdesk ticket?* Or, *Describe your process for handling escalations from beginning to end?* Our carefully structured meetings lasted all day. We returned to the office with reams of new insights that shaped our understanding of the customer's world.

Must you use all these techniques to determine your best point of competitive differentiation and positioning? Not at all. Each business is unique, and depending on what knowledge you already have, you'll know which of these techniques will be most helpful to hone your competitive differentiation.

---17---

POSITIONING STATEMENTS IN ACTION

In summary, use the following cheat sheet in Table 6 for guiding teams through the positioning statement exercise.

POSITIONING STATEMENT CRITERIA
1) Is there a clear target audience/persona? Is the target singular and specific?
2) Does the category exist? Does the product name and category fit together?
3) Is the benefit singular and specific?
4) Is the benefit relevant?
5) Is the benefit sustainable?
6) Is the benefit believable?
7) Can you substantiate the benefit?
8) Is there a clear, defensible product differentiator?

Table 6: A criteria to help evaluate positioning statements

Working the positioning statement exercise is more art than science, and the output is somewhat subjective. As you review these examples illustrated in Figures 12, 13, and 14, refer to the cheat sheet. What aspects are clear? Where might you provide refinements? While these are real positioning statements, the names of the companies and products have been removed to protect their confidentiality.

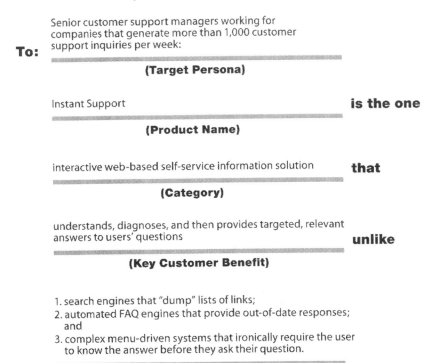

To: Senior customer support managers working for companies that generate more than 1,000 customer support inquiries per week:

(Target Persona)

Instant Support   **is the one**

(Product Name)

interactive web-based self-service information solution   **that**

(Category)

understands, diagnoses, and then provides targeted, relevant answers to users' questions   **unlike**

(Key Customer Benefit)

1. search engines that "dump" lists of links;
2. automated FAQ engines that provide out-of-date responses; and
3. complex menu-driven systems that ironically require the user to know the answer before they ask their question.

(Nearest Competitive Alternative)

Figure 12: A positioning statement for a knowledge management company. This positioning statement was developed in 2000, before search engines became a component of just about every online interaction.

Pros:

- *This statement is very easy to read and understand. Upon reading it, every marketer and sales rep understood it and could repeat it.*

- *The target audience is not "everyone." Even with this short description, the reader can get a sense of what companies might be included In the target list.*
- *There are three competitive alternatives listed, each highlighting a shortcoming. This gives the marketer a foundation for some interesting messaging angles.*

Cons:

- *The biggest risk here is regarding a sustainable benefit. As technology improves, the marketer needs to be very careful to constantly update the positioning strategy to stay relevant and not be seen as "old school" or out of touch.*

To: CEOs, CIOs, and office managers of mid-sized businesses

(Target Persona)

(Company name) **is the one**

(Product Name)

single-source, Unified Communications-as-a-Service (UCaaS) company offering an integrated suite of best-of breed communications services and equipment **that**

(Category)

improves employee productivity by providing the latest "find me, follow me" phone, email, and texting applications accessible through a web interface with customizable routing options **unlike**

(Key Customer Benefit)

high-maintenance, home-grown PBX communications networks that are based on old technology and overburden your IT team with tactical issues instead of allowing them to focus on more strategic priorities.

(Nearest Competitive Alternative)

Figure 13: A positioning statement for a telecommunications company

Pros:
- *This is also a nice, simple statement.*
- *In this case, the product and the company are essentially the same. A start-up with limited funds needs to decide on where to establish its brand. Here, focusing at the company level made sense.*
- *The benefit is "improves productivity," and rather than leaving that statement vague, they include a description of how productivity is improved. This gives proper context.*
- *The main competitor here isn't actually another company; it's the "status quo," where these companies attempt to build their own solutions on top of the products they already have.*

Cons:
- *The weakness here is with the target-audience description. We need more information about the buyer. An accompanying persona would provide key information about the CEOs and CIOs, their priorities, concerns, and preferences*
- *They are trying to establish a new category of "Unified Communications as a Service" company. Do these words make sense to potential buyers? For early adopters, probably so. For the general business market, not sure. Some careful market investment may be required to educate the target audience on this new category and why they should care.*

To: IT leaders responsible for synchronizing IT to support business needs (The "skeptical futurist" persona):

(Target Persona)

(Company name)   **is the one**

(Product Name)

single-vendor and strategic partner that can provide a comprehensive network architecture tailored for business agility, combining both unified wired and wireless products **that**

(Category)

gives you confidence in designing and implementing a flexible, future-proof network access strategy that will lower operational expenses and enable business collaboration while enforcing security and compliance **unlike**

(Key Customer Benefit)

1. Competitor X that pushes point products at the expense of the broader network infrastructure;
2. Competitor Y that is distracted with a new acquisition and whose network access roadmap is unsettled; and
3. Competitor Z that has a limited product family and introduces risk by not having an architecture approach.

(Nearest Competitive Alternative)

Figure 14: A positioning statement for a networking company

Pros:

- *This team constructed a persona they called "The Skeptical Futurist." This became a handy reference shared widely amongst the team.*
- *As in Figure 12, this team also chose to position the company and not a specific product. They determined that the target audience prioritized the need to feel confident in making a good purchase decision as being more important than the actual hardware being purchased. Thus, the category choice became "single vendor, strategic partner." The confidence angle plays well to their brand image, so they chose to lead with*

that. This is a helpful reminder that competing feature-to-feature isn't always required or appropriate.

- *Three competitive alternatives are offered here, each revealing a weakness that could be exploited in the messaging.*

Cons:

- *The category and benefit elements are rather verbose. This isn't necessarily a bad thing because the positioning statement is not the message to customers. However, it is critical that every word be meaningful to the marketing team. Watch out for streams of technical jargon that ramble on and muddle the intention.*

- *The differentiators against the three nearest competitive alternatives are written from an internal perspective. But are these really true, or just complaints based on gossip? As marketing is really aimed at managing perceptions, these statements are acceptable. However, it is probably worthwhile to explore these in more detail to see if they are meaningful to the intended personas. Some additional market research would be helpful to substantiate these statements.*

- *As a central positioning statement, addressing the top three competitors here serves a purpose. However, these specific differentiators are only relevant when competitor X, Y, and Z are engaged with the prospect. And each of these differentiators is likely to be relevant in the short-term only. If we assume them to be true (as per the bullet point above), then time is of the essence to make use of them now. They are not sustainable.*

_____18_____

GETTING TO THE HIGH GROUND

The point of the positioning statement exercise is to understand the customers and to determine how to best relate to them. What separates the best, most effective marketers from the rest? The answer lies in their ability to know the customers and what makes them tick better than anyone else. They've captured the marketing high ground.

Most companies have small armies of folks who understand the product, the technology, and the applications. This is absolutely required for success. However, many companies lose site of the customer, the use cases, and their drivers and needs. Without a firm understanding of what the customer cares about and how he or she makes purchase decisions, marketers don't have a leg to stand on when debating peers and executives who passionately propose new (seemingly random) creative features or marketing gimmicks. If marketing teams invest in gaining knowledge found in the marketing high ground, over time, their opinions are more likely to be sought out rather than ignored. So, how does one get to the marketing high ground? While marketing teams don't always have the luxury of a deep budget for conducting ongoing market research, there are some guerilla tactics that can be employed.

- ***Review any existing primary and secondary research.*** *You may have more than you think you have because market research is often conducted in a silo fashion, meaning that one department may not proactively share its research with another. Check around with your PR and product-marketing colleagues. See what they've collected.*
- ***If you have a subscription with any analysts, take advantage of researching their library.*** *Also, conduct Internet searches to find out what other analysts and editors are writing about.*
- ***Review relevant blogs, Wikis, and other Internet sources for everything from related trends to customer feedback.*** *Don't forget to check YouTube: competitors as well as customers and other influencers sometimes go to great lengths to show competitive comparisons. You need to know if, how, and when they are talking about your products and services.*
- ***Talk to your own sales reps, sales engineers, and customer support specialists.*** *Find out what customers and prospects are saying to them. Instead of gathering internal data one rep at a time, go one step further to design a short, survey or questionnaire for your internal teammates. Collect and quantify this data.*
- ***Analyze competitor websites and message boards.*** *Find out what they're talking about and how prospects are interacting with them.*

Preparing for your journey

Owning the marketing high ground doesn't happen over night. It takes time. And it is a never-ending process.

1. *Establish a repository of this customer knowledge that the marketing team can share with sales.*
2. *Take fifteen minutes every other day to learn something new about your customers and how/why you won their business.*
3. *When making your case, always reference sources of information.* Don't lead with "I think . . ." Starting a debate this way makes it personal. Instead, start with "Based on customer insight and data we've collected . . ." Your actions and position should show that you empathize with the customer. Use those insights to reinforce your recommendations.
4. *Look for opportunities to share and socialize your draft positioning statements.* Building solid positioning statements is a team sport, not an activity for an individual.

Share, communicate, evangelize

Everyone from the CEO to the guy working the mailroom needs to know what the positioning statement is and what it means. A lot of data, debate, and discussion go into crafting the positioning statement. While only a few people working the process need to know the finer details behind each carefully chosen word, everyone should have the final positioning statement slide at his or her fingertips. Guy Kawasaki states this imperative beautifully in his book, *The Art of the Start:* "Crafting the positioning of an organization is a demanding process, but well worth the effort. It's a pity that many companies get to this point and then do nothing more than send out a halfhearted internal memo or stick a rote positioning statement in an annual report. For shame."[15]

Understanding a company's or a product's positioning is critical for all employees. Regardless of the title of the job they hold, every employee is also a marketing-arm and a sales-representative for the company. If they don't understand the positioning, if they can't translate it into effective product designs and clear messaging, then how can customers and prospects ever hope to understand it? Communicate it internally early and often to keep it fresh and top of mind in all employees.

If you follow this approach consistently, you will build more credibility for your programs and for yourself as a tuned-in marketer. And, the next time an executive does a fly-by, you can engage in a more constructive debate allowing you to leverage more detailed, documented information to support and defend your product roadmaps and integrated marketing campaigns.

Part Three: PERSUASION

The most effective technique for crafting customer-ready messages

"People don't want more information. They are up to their eyeballs in information. They want faith—faith in you, your goals, your success, in the story you tell."[16]

Annette Simmons, author and story-telling expert

_____19_____

MAPPING CUSTOMER PERCEPTION

Before we dive into messaging, we need to take a slight detour and review how people make purchase decisions, especially those weighty purchase decisions that are made for businesses, involve multiple team players, and carry a big price tag. Those buyers typically engage in a buying process similar to the one shown in Figure 15. The typical B2B technology customer buying process starts with an operational analysis and investment planning, which transitions into a purchasing cycle where various alternatives are considered, and ultimately concludes with a purchase decision and implementation.

The challenge for marketers is to aim the message at the right person, at the right time, during the buying process, and via the right media. The buyer needs to hear the message in time to consider the product. That's the only way the sales rep will have a chance of winning the sale. But mindlessly blasting only the "Buy Now!" horn over and over again will fail to engage the buyer. The message will go unheard or unheeded.

Buyers of technology products routinely go through a process of built-in checks and balances to guide decision-making. It starts with an assessment of a problem or opportunity that needs addressing. With a business case made and approval to proceed, the buyer engages in the purchasing cycle. The steps generalized in the purchase cycle may happen very quickly, or they may take months, depending on the complexity or associated costs of the problem or technology

Figure 15: A generic buying process used by technology companies

being addressed. Ultimately a variety of vendors will be considered with a few being invited to bid on the project. Only after careful scrutiny will a vendor be selected and the solution implemented. While this process appears simple and clinical, it usually involves many reviewers and influencers who contribute to a recommendation made to the final decision-maker.

But what's going on inside the head of the targeted buyer?

A variety of content and information will be sought at each stage of the buying process. This provides opportunities for the marketer to engage with the buyer at each stage of the buying process. Let's unveil the buying process a bit. Before the buyer makes a purchase decision he or she needs to be **aware** of all of the possible alternatives, and the buyer will only pursue those options that **interest** him or her, and purchase decisions will be guided by those options that are the most credible and offer the best value. This drives **preference**. The able-bodied marketer must deliver a whole series of messages *before* the purchase **decision** is made. This is illustrated in the communications objectives flow represented above the buying process illustrated in Figure 16.

It is not a coincidence that awareness messages work most effectively if the buyer hears them early in the purchase process. If we can hook the buyer while she is establishing the need, building an information technology (IT) project, and forming a Request for Quote (RFQ), then we've successfully made a connection. The marketer's goal is to offer valuable, relevant content when the buyer is ready to receive it. Then she will be more likely to raise her hand and say, *"tell me more!"* When marketers continue to nurture the relationship through the purchase cycle by offering additional, meaningful information and evidence, then the marketer can influence the buyer, encouraging her to prefer their product over competing alternatives. The chance of a successful sale increases exponentially if our messages can unfold in this way,

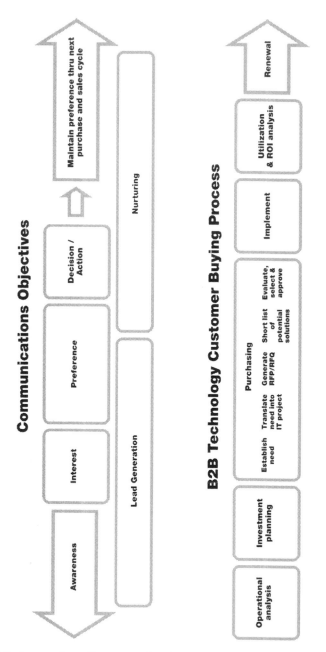

Figure 16: An overlay of communications objectives to the customer's buying process reveals opportunities for influencing customer perception.

like chapters In a book. Success requires patience in how and when we engage prospects. Pushing too much information too soon or information out of sequence will just be interpreted as noise.

There's one more piece we need to add to this puzzle: the sales process. The purpose of marketing is to help sales sell. As such, the marketer needs to produce sales tools that will help sales reps follow-up on leads and nurture them to a conclusion. With this in mind, we can add the final piece to our mapping exercise: the B2B direct sales process, as illustrated in Figure 17.

In sales terms, this is called the "complex sale." In the complex sale, these messages (building awareness, creating interest, driving preference, prompting a decision) evolve over time. In impulse purchases, they may happen all at once. But it's the former that we'll focus on here. There are a number of excellent books on the complex sales process, and I won't dwell here to repeat the finer points other than to refer you to these books:

- Jeff Thull, *Mastering the Complex Sale*, John Wiley & Sons, Inc, 2010
- Brian Carroll, *Lead Generation and the Complex Sale*, McGraw-Hill, 2006
- Rick Page, *Hope is not a Sales Strategy: the Six Keys to Winning the Complex Sale*, McGraw-Hill, 2003

The bottom line: messaging is not about the manufacturer. It's about the buyer, their priorities, and the problems they are trying to solve. As such, buyers are looking for different types of information at different times during their buying process. We, as marketers, need to understand the process and the type of information these folks are looking for. And we need to deliver this content in a format and venue they will welcome. Marketing automation tools, such as Marketo, Eloqua, and Silverpop help streamline the process. The better

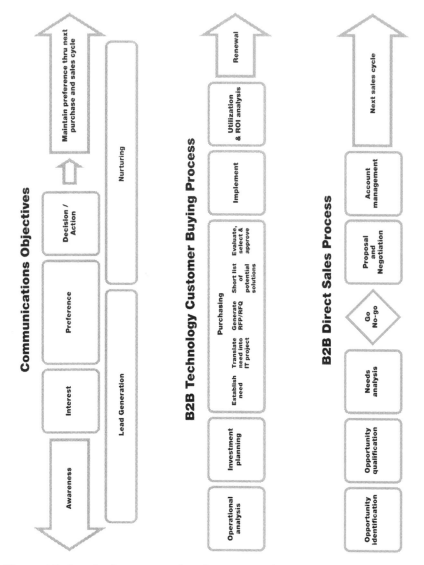

Figure 17: Overlaying a generic sales process for the "complex sale"[17]

we understand how these three processes overlap and link, the more relevant and targeted our messages will be. Success will be measured in the dialog we nurture and conversion rates we receive. And we won't be wasting time and money on marketing messages that are irrelevant or ill timed.

20

NOBODY WANTS TO BE SOLD TO

The act of "selling" brings to mind the stereotypical example of the crass used-car salesman, decked out in his best plaid suit, shouting messages at you. All you wanted to do was browse, and bam! He's in your face.

It is a cliché, but it's true: the Internet changed everything. We, as buyers, are savvier because of the Internet. We do our own research. In fact, I'll go out on a limb to say that most people use the Internet to *avoid* the sales rep. We seek information, product reviews, testimonials in secret, hoping that the sales rep won't notice us. Until, that is, we are ready to be found. Buyers today are in control of their buying process and, by extension, they control how and when marketers and sales reps can engage them. This single fact changes the way marketers must think about going to market.

The days of mass marketing, and even niche marketing are over. Today, buyers want to engage on their own terms, in a one-on-one fashion. That means our marketing campaigns, programs, activities, and offers need to be geared to speak to an individual, not a mob, not a group. But if people don't want to be sold to, how should we engage them? The answer is through story telling.

Businesses selling to consumers (B2C) understood the power of storytelling years ago. Consider the commercials for Tide that tells stories about people who get their clothes dirty and need a solution to get them to be as clean as new.

The message is not just "Buy Tide!" The message is a story that illustrates a life situation that buyers can relate to. The consumer hears it, sees it, and can say, *"Hey, that applies to me."*

Traditionally, businesses selling to businesses (B2B) have been stuck in a rut of developing messages all about them or their technologies. Many businesses today follow the messaging approach used by Bette Midler in the 1988 movie, *Beaches.* Her famous line: *"But enough about me, let's talk about you...what do you think about me?"*

Unfortunately, B2B messages are more likely to be about features or technologies, not benefits. Or they're egocentric messages like, "Buy from us. We've been in business for fifty years!"

Now, there is a time and a place in the selling process for messages like these; however, this is not an effective way to start a dialog. To be draconian, let me suggest that prospects and customers don't care about your business goals, your technology, whether your solution is "open source" or not, or what you personally think is "cool" about your product. What she cares about is herself and specifically, the problem she is trying to solve. If your product or service can help her solve their problem, then we've got a connection. If not, she'll pass you by like a rush-hour commuter focused on exiting a crowded subway.

The good news is that many marketers and the companies they work for are starting to recognize the value of story telling. But how do you do it? And how do you engage a skeptical organization to change its messaging approach when it's used to promoting "me, me, me" messaging?

I've used a dozen different messaging techniques over the past twenty-five years. While they all had the goal of helping my team separate the yogurt from the watery stuff that sits on top, there is only one technique that I believe in today. Only one technique has helped me consistently develop customer-ready messaging. It's called the message box. I learned the message box concept from Susan Thomas and Tobey Fitch, two marketing leaders who understand the psychology of buyer behavior.

The origins of the concept of story telling are actually a time-honored tool for media trainers who need to keep their spokespersons on message. "It's especially effective when you have someone who tends to wander in his or her answers and stray off message," Susan explained.

I've applied variations of this technique in a hundred different situations: from selling software solutions, hardware products, and even promoting non-profits. Here's what it is, how it works, and why it continues to make a difference to a growing population of marketers everywhere.

—————————————21—————————————

INTRODUCING THE MESSAGE BOX

Successful selling is about story telling. And our messaging must tell a story that is relevant to our target personae. But what makes a good story? Let's take a page from literature, literally. A good, engaging book, whether it's *A Christmas Carol* by Charles Dickens, *Harry Potter and the Deathly Hallows* by J.K. Rowling, or *Pillars of the Earth* by Ken Follett, all follow a similar, simple pattern:

1. *Something happens to upset the status quo, creating dramatic tension and provoking an emotional response.*
2. *Our hero works to restore balance.*
3. *Ultimately, our hero prevails.*
4. *Life returns to normal or better than normal.*

This same formula also works for creating an engaging *business story*, with some slight modifications. A good business story:

1. *engages the persona (our hero) by describing a problem they are experiencing and creating dramatic tension;*

2. *offers a criteria for a compelling solution, or key success factors that the hero must meet regardless of the vendor to be selected;*

3. *introduces our product as being the best able to meet this criteria, including specific benefits, features, and evidence, making our solution credible to the persona; and*

4. *describes the value of our solution in terms of outcome, specifically illustrating how the hero's life is now normal again or better than before.*

That's it. It seems surprisingly simple. However, don't be fooled. The secret to developing messaging that will ring true to the target persona takes practice. The message box technique is illustrated in Figure 18.

This is the most creative, fun, and simplest technique I've found to craft a company's or product's story, and it works equally well for B2B, B2C, and even non-profit organizations. It's universal because we're engaging a persona on a personal level. Remember, it is people with needs, desires, and fears who buy products, not faceless companies.

Message box outputs

There are two outputs derived from the message box exercise:

1) The elevator pitch

You're at a cocktail party and someone politely asks you, "Tell me about your new product." He's looking for a short response that answers this question. What do you say? Do you start with a history lesson, as one executive did to me: "Well, twenty years ago . . ." Boring. Do you babble on for ten minutes, hoping to sound intelligent? Cringe. Marketers need a crisp story that everyone can speak to with confidence.

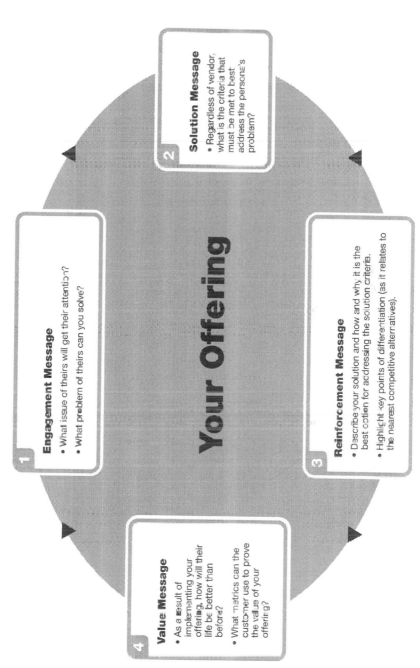

Figure 18: The message box is a tool for story telling.[18]

They need an elevator pitch—a short story they can quickly communicate, as if the only time they had with the customer was the length of a short elevator ride. And that is what this technique represents. While our story is short and sweet, it is purposely not complete. Too much information will only work against us. It doesn't need to include a laundry list of features or an education of the technology involved. That comes later in a nurtured dialog. The sole goal of the message box is to produce a short, crisp opener that is relevant to the target audience. We want them to lean forward and respond, "Tell me more!" Those three little words are an invitation to delve deeper in conversation.

2) A message map

Once we have outlined our story in the message box, we can look for opportunities to expand each message during the course of the dialog with the prospect. Each of the four messages becomes a theme for additional dialog. Each theme may have multiple messages that support it. This provides an excellent outline for scripting the dialog that can be used to nurture prospects through the buying process. For example, most companies have an abundance of product messages (based on key features) but may be shy in value messages (i.e., customer testimonials) or engagement messages (i.e., business problems customers face). By mapping the messages to the buying process, marketers can focus their efforts to develop messages that fill in the gaps. Figure 19 illustrates where the four messages fit.

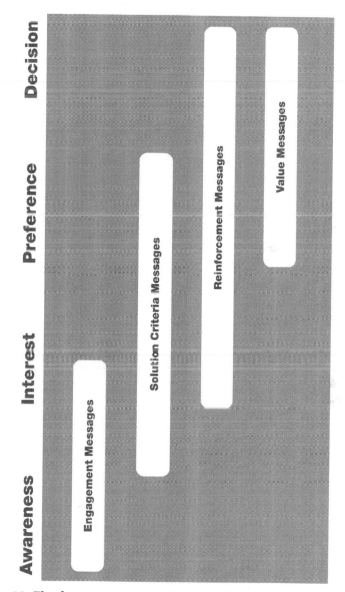

Figure 19: The four messages outlined in the message box become themes for content used in different phases of the buying process.

22

HOW AND WHY THE MESSAGE BOX WORKS

As a bunch, we collective marketers are driven to take action. We have deliverables to produce, advertising copy to write, websites to update. However, be warned: when marketers attempt to write messages and copy without a clear understanding of the target persona and the core positioning, the messages will be less than optimal. It's possible that the ad copy may be punchy, and you may feel you've earned your pay, but you may have inadvertently lengthened the sales cycle because your messages, as creative as they are, are not in sync with the larger story. Worse, your messages may actually be irrelevant to the target buyer. If you already have at least a draft hypothesis of the target persona and a prioritization of the benefits you can provide them, then you are ready to write your copy. If not, rally a team of co-conspirators and take an hour to put your best guess forward. If you need more help, I highly recommend taking advantage of a skilled marketing facilitator who can guide you through the woods and alert you when you fall into the traps of hype, jargon, and nonsensical corporate speak.

There are six components to the message box.

1) The persona

Everything world-class marketers produce is geared toward the persona. The conscientious marketer is the customer's/prospect's advocate. So, the first thing to do is to include the name of the persona in the upper left-hand corner. Use the three-word label that resulted from the persona exercise. Remember "The Skeptical Futurist?" This acts as a shorthand reminder for the team. We'll be able to evaluate our messages as being relevant (or not) against the backdrop of this persona.

2) The center box

The message box is so called, because it acts as a visual reminder that we are trying to sell a specific product, service, or company. That "thing" is represented in the box, center to this template. Write in the name of the "thing" you are trying to promote. The product, such as "Apple MacBook Pro" or "EMC Premium Support," or the company: "Cisco" or "Startup XYZ."

Now, things get interesting, as the messages unfold around the center box. Let's start at the top and move clockwise.

3) Message 1 = the engagement message

This represents the *hook* that will capture our persona's attention. We can craft this message as either a statement or a question. It doesn't matter. What does matter is that we speak the persona's language. How do they describe their problem, opportunity, or interest? We need to use the same words and engage them by painting a picture of an issue they are care about (*one that we can solve—although they don't know that yet!*) The engagement message is all about them. Not you. Your company name does not appear here; your product name does not appear here, either. You'll introduce your solution in message 3. (Hint: remember the problem, need, fear factor, or pet peeves illustrated as part of your persona? Find a way to replay that key information as the hook.)

4) Message 2 = the "solution criteria" message

Contrary to what you are probably thinking, this "solution" message is *not* about you. Again, consider the solution from the persona's viewpoint. They have a problem that needs to be solved. There are any number of choices and alternatives available to them. How will they decide what to consider? Inevitably, they will have (or will develop) a criteria checklist. Regardless of which vendor they select, they will have a set of conditions that must be met. Sure, there are trade-offs to be considered. But in the perfect world, the checklist will act as their agenda. And you want to be on it. So, the solution message is your opportunity to exercise some "thought leadership" and suggest to the persona what criteria she should be considering. Don't make this a long list. Too much information kills the message box. Limit the list to three things—three things that are of critical importance to the persona, and three things that you can slam-dunk the competition on. (Hint: remember the benefits and competitive differentiation you drafted in the positioning statement? Use that here.)

5) Message 3 = the product reinforcement message

You've been waiting for this, and here it is. Introduce your company and your product here. You've already set the context. Now, this is your opportunity to state why your product or service is the best for meeting the solution criteria indicated in message 2. Describe your solution, briefly, and indicate a couple of points of differentiation, as it relates to the nearest competitive alternative. (Hint: this needs to be a short message, not a data sheet filled with numbers and jargon. What is the one-liner about your product that you want the persona to remember?)

6) Message 4 = the value message

This is where you tell the persona how and why their life will be back to normal or better than normal, as a result of using your product or service. If you have relevant metrics on use cases and customer successes, play that information here. (Hint: making use of customer references, third-party endorsements, and evidence culled from side-by-side product comparisons can be very powerful here.)

_____23_____

THE MESSAGE BOX IN ACTION

Each of the following stories represents a real product from a real company and how each used the message box to tighten their messaging.

Story 1: It's miserable to fly and you know it!
This is a story about a frequent-flyer business executive. Most flyers will tell you that the allure of travel around the world is energizing and awe-inspiring. At least at first. But after multiple trips, many taken back-to-back, flight travel begins to be not so glamorous. Fighting fatigue and jet lag is a real problem. To address this problem, the entrepreneur I worked with developed an all-natural cure for jet lag. His story is told in Figure 20. While this isn't a B2B story, per se, the persona is that of a very busy business executive. This is something that all business people can relate to, no matter how often we travel ourselves.

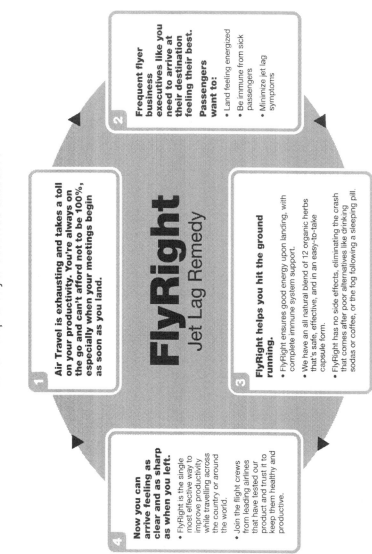

STORY: It's miserable to fly and you know it!

Persona: Frequent flyer business executive

FlyRight
Jet Lag Remedy

1. Air Travel is exhausting and takes a toll on your productivity. You're always on the go and can't afford not to be 100%, especially when your meetings begin as soon as you land.

2. Frequent flyer business executives like you need to arrive at their destination feeling their best.

Passengers want to:
- Land feeling energized
- Be immune from sick passengers
- Minimize jet lag symptoms

3. FlyRight helps you hit the ground running.
- FlyRight ensures good energy upon landing, with complete immune system support.
- We have an all natural blend of 12 organic herbs that's safe, effective, and in an easy-to-take capsule form.
- FlyRight has no side effects, eliminating the crash that comes after poor alternatives like drinking sodas or coffee, or the fog following a sleeping pill.

4. Now you can arrive feeling as clear and as sharp as when you left.
- FlyRight is the single most effective way to improve productivity while travelling across the country or around the world.
- Join the flight crews from leading airlines that have tested our product and trust it to keep them healthy and productive.

Figure 20: FlyRight's message box reflects an easy to understand story.[19]

Observations:
1. *There are many things the entrepreneur could have used to begin his story. He chose to go with the "productivity" theme after interviewing a number of business travelers. This theme echoes throughout each of the four messages.*

2. *The solution message (message #2) is designed to list criteria that the frequent-flyer business executive cares about. No doubt this criteria may also appeal to other travelers. That's okay. If other audiences like the criteria, then the entrepreneur will gladly sell his product to them, too. What's most important, however, is establishing criteria the persona cares about and that the product can address.*

3. *Notice that his branded product name does not appear in the engagement message or the solution message. Those first two messages must be all about the persona. Marketers use those messages to establish a common bond with the persona and to show that they really do understand the problems he or she faces. It is in the reinforcement message that we first introduce the product. This is where the marketer shows how and why the product is best able to meet the criteria discussed earlier. Also, you will notice several competitive comparisons in this message. In the entrepreneur's investigation, he found that his primary competitor was not another jet lag remedy, per se; it was common products like coffee, sodas, or sleeping pills.*

4. *Lastly, the value message is the reciprocal of the engagement message. To paraphrase: the engagement message is about air travel taking a toll on productivity; the value message reveals that productivity need not suffer when air travelers use his jet lag remedy.*

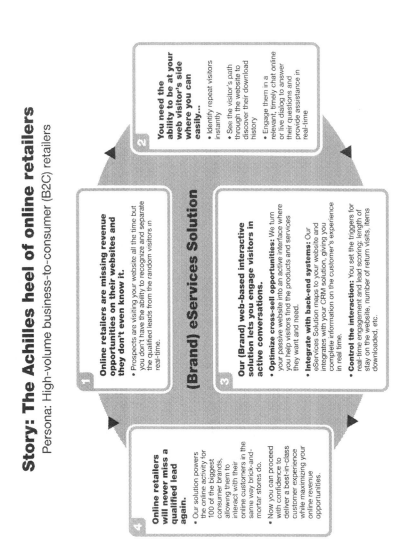

Story: The Achilles heel of online retailers

Persona: High-volume business-to-consumer (B2C) retailers

1

Online retailers are missing revenue opportunities on their websites and they don't even know it.

• Prospects are visiting your website all the time but you don't have the ability to recognize and separate the qualified leads from the random visitors in real-time.

2

You need the ability to be at your web visitor's side where you can easily...

• Identify repeat visitors instantly

• See the visitor's path through the website to discover their download history

• Engage them in a relevant, timely chat online or live dialog to answer their questions and provide assistance in real-time

(Brand) eServices Solution

3

Our (Brand) web-based interactive solution lets you engage visitors in active conversations.

• **Optimize cross-sell opportunities:** We turn your passive website into an active interface where you help visitors find the products and services they want and need.

• **Integrate with back-end systems:** Our eServices Solution maps to your website and integrates with your CRM solution, giving you complete information on the customer's experience in real time.

• **Control the interaction:** You set the triggers for real-time engagement and lead scoring: length of stay on the website, number of return visits, items downloaded, etc.

4

Online retailers will never miss a qualified lead again.

• Our solution powers the online activity for 100 of the biggest consumer brands, allowing them to interact with their online customers in the same way brick-and-mortar stores do.

• Now you can proceed with confidence to deliver a best-in-class customer experience while maximizing your online revenue opportunities.

Figure 21: A message box for online retailers.[20] The message box is also a helpful tool for guiding discussions on product use case scenarios.

Story 2: The Achilles heel of online retailers

Figure 21 is a story about call-center managers who run high-volume B2C retail stores. They are responsible for driving sales in their brick and mortar stores as well as via their commerce websites. At the time this message box exercise was conducted, websites were largely static and one-dimensional: while consumers could make purchases online, there was no opportunity for the retailer and visitor to engage in a dialog. A VP of product management used the message box technique to rally his team in building a series of product-use cases around this story.

Observations:

1. *This engagement message is a very bold statement. To grab attention they were willing to be a bit controversial in making this claim. The beauty of this approach is that no matter what the prospect's reaction is, the hook has been planted and a dialog will unfold. Consider that if the prospect agrees ("What! I had no idea. What do you mean?"), or if she takes issue ("You're wrong! We are in complete control . . ."), the sales rep has identified the prospect's stance. He can now tailor his dialog with her accordingly. The point of the engagement message is to engage the prospect. It is not required that the prospect agree with the message.*

2. *Moving forward in the dialog, the sales rep can explain the criteria required to maximize revenue opportunities on the website. If the prospect is receptive, the conversation can continue in more detail.*

3. *As noted in Story 1, the product's name is not introduced until the reinforcement message. In this case, the story provides three top-line features that begin to build interest and credibility regarding the product.*

4. *Finally, the value message reveals a direct response to the engagement message.*

Story 3: Do you know what your customers are talking about?

The story about customer support managers working at companies that experience large volumes of customer traffic and feedback is illustrated in Figure 22. With the advent of social media, customers are talking about a company's products in a variety of formats—some on the company's website and customer surveys, and some in unstructured chat rooms, Twitter, user-group forums, and other venues that the company does not control. This is the age of the empowered consumer, and they have the ability to influence a company's bottom line like never before.

Consider what Charlene Li and Josh Bernoff write in their book, *Groundswell*: "Right now, your customers are writing about your products on blogs and recutting your commercials on YouTube. They're defining you on Wikipedia and ganging up on you on social networking sites like Facebook. These are all elements of a social phenomenon—the groundswell—that has created a permanent shift in the way the world works."[21]

To build relevance, a start-up company called Overtone capitalizes on social media trends to make its business case more imperative to prospects.

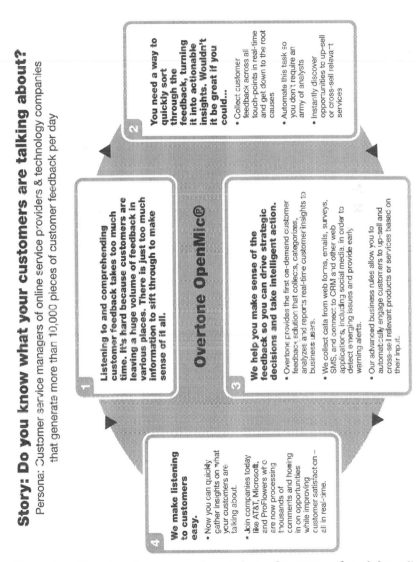

Story: Do you know what your customers are talking about?

Persona: Customer service managers of online service providers & technology companies that generate more than 10,000 pieces of customer feedback per day

2. You need a way to quickly sort through the feedback, turning it into actionable insights. Wouldn't it be great if you could...

- Collect customer feedback across all touch-points in real-time and get down to the root causes
- Automate this task so you don't require an army of analysts
- Instantly discover opportunities to up-sell or cross-sell relevant services

1. Listening to and comprehending customer feedback takes too much time. It's hard because customers are leaving a huge volume of feedback in various places. There is just too much information to sift through to make sense of it all.

Overtone OpenMic®

3. We help you make sense of the feedback so you can drive strategic decisions and take intelligent action.

- Overtone provides the first on-demand customer feedback solution that collects, categorizes, analyzes and reports real-time customer insights to business users.
- We collect data from web forms, emails, surveys, SMS, and connect to CRM and other web applications, including social media in order to detect emerging issues and provide early warning alerts.
- Our advanced business rules allow you to automatically engage customers to up-sell and cross-sell relevant products or services based on their input.

4. We make listening to customers easy.

- Now you can quickly gather insights on what your customers are talking about.
- Join companies today like AT&T, Microsoft, and ProFlowers who are now processing thousands of comments and honing in on opportunities while improving customer satisfaction — all in real-time.

Figure 22: Overtone's message box takes advantage of social media trends to make its business case.[22]

Observations:

1. *The engagement message is designed to provoke an emotional response. The upshot: there is just too much customer feedback to sift through to make sense of it all! Yet not to try is an invitation to disaster that may befall your company at any instant.*

2. *The solution message illustrates a set of criteria against which any and all solutions should be evaluated. Of course, this list is not comprehensive. Remember, it is not our goal to deliver a thesis via the message box. All we want to do is engage the prospect so they respond, "Tell me more." Then, we are given the invitation to delve further into the relevant topics, conditions, and benefits.*

3. *Similarly, the reinforcement is not the data sheet. The message box requires focus on which key benefits and features are the most important to play first.*

4. *And finally, the value message is so simple that anyone can understand it.*

24

HIERARCHY OF MESSAGING

The message box is an excellent exercise for developing an elevator pitch, as we've just discussed. However, before we start rattling off our messages, there is a related framework to consider: a message hierarchy, as shown in Figure 23.

Years ago, while working on a product launch, my team ran into some messaging trouble. Our task was to introduce a *new* product to a *new* market segment and steal market share. This task was clear enough. Yet we struggled to understand why our marketing efforts weren't getting enough traction. After a dismal quarter, we stepped back to do a complete post mortem on our launch activities. The problem we found was with our messaging.

1. *While our product was well received in market segment A, segment B had no idea who we were (even though we thought they did).*
2. *When we did an impromptu segment B focus group, we found they were confused and disbelieving of our messages. Thus, they ignored them.*

The team was incredulous. After all, we were one of the biggest companies around. To solve our problem, we had to check our egos at the door and re-focus on the business problem the prospects were trying to solve. After much

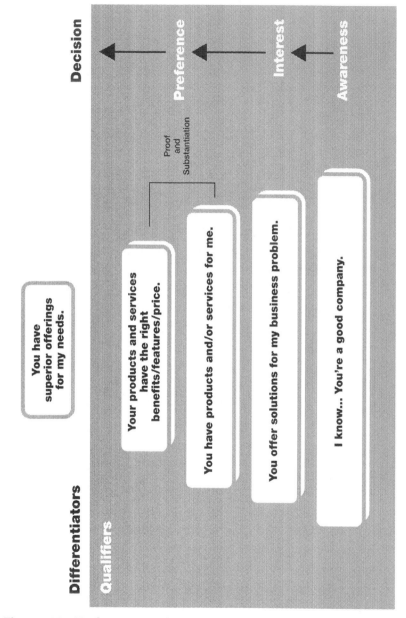

Figure 23: Marketers need to guide the target audiences up the messaging pyramid. To jump to the close (i.e. the differentiator) before establishing awareness, interest, or preference first (i.e. the qualifiers) will only lead to confusion because the persona won't understand what you are talking about.

gnashing of teeth, we realized that we couldn't just go for the quick sale. We needed to invest time with the new segments in order to earn the right to sell to them.

We needed to establish awareness and relevance for our company in segment B. This qualified us in the minds of our prospects. Only then did we have an invitation to compare our new product with the various incumbents. And only then could we promote our differentiators with confidence.

To keep us on track, we produced a message hierarchy chart similar to the one shown in Figure 23. This kept us humble and helped us define a winning marketing blueprint that worked. Six months later, when we reintroduced the product we had a much more favorable response.

_____25_____

MESSAGE KILLERS

The following list of message killers represents the most common weak points found in messaging.[23] When marketers fall victim to just one of these, there is great risk to the credibility of the message. Suffer from multiple afflictions and the message is surely to be viewed with disdain, if not ignored entirely.

- *Complex messages, too many words when a few will do*
- *Jargon or buzzwords only understood by a few*
- *Unsubstantiated claims that assume too much*
- *Overly clinical, bland with an academic insistence on precision*
- *Hyperbole and (unfounded) exaggerated claims*
- *"It's all about me"*

Upon completing your draft message box and message hierarchy, critique them against this list of message killers. How well do they rate?

Part Four: ENGAGEMENT

How to conduct these exercises for best success

"Teamwork is the ability to work together toward a common vision. The ability to direct individual accomplishments toward organizational objectives. It is the fuel that allows common people to attain uncommon results. [24]

Andrew Carnegie, American industrialist, businessman, entrepreneur

_____26_____

WORKING THE EXERCISES

What's the best way to put these tools and techniques to use? The answer depends on whether you are a team member in a global marketing department or if you are the jack-of-all-trades marketer working in a small company or start-up. While the best practices and templates apply equally in either case, how you use them internally will be different. In the pages that follow, I share agendas, tips, and techniques that can be applied.

Let's face it; your time is limited. People are distracted with many duties in their daily jobs. As such, it can be difficult to get quality mind-share from team members. And, typically, people don't like to be "trained." To engage folks, I've found that conducting "working sessions" is an excellent way to bring people together to tackle a common goal. Whereas "workshops" connote training exercises that are academic in nature and invite skepticism from participants who may be unsure how to apply the concepts, "working sessions" are opportunities to get real work done. The output is achieved faster, and the team gets to experiment with these techniques in real time. It's a win-win, and the team's skill level has been advanced without them even knowing it!

Positioning and messaging go hand-in-hand, and the journey to the marketing high ground begins with understanding the target audience: the persona. While the persona and bulls-eye segmentation, positioning statement, and message box exercises can be applied in an ad hoc fashion, the best results are achieved when they are linked together and tackled in the order presented in this book.

Regardless of the size of company you work in, engaging in these techniques requires careful thought and a time commitment. Table 7 provides a perspective of a generic agenda and a typical time allotment. Of course, you may find you need more or less time, depending on the sophistication of your organization and the knowledge of the market, target buyer, and product you already possess. Regardless, this is a good starting point for companies large or small.

If you are able to sequester a cross-functional marketing and sales team for a day, you can quickly make a lot of progress. However, the agenda can be applied with equal success when broken into two or three smaller sessions. Let's break it down.

AGENDA ITEMS	TIME
1. Setting the context for this working session	15 minutes
2. Segmentation prioritization via the bull's eye exercise	30 - 60 minutes
3. Illustrating the persona	30 - 60 minutes
4. Designing the positioning statement	1 - 3 hours
5. Drafting the message box	1 - 3 hours
6. Identify next steps for socializing the output	20 minutes

Table 7: A typical agenda can be worked in a single day, or broken down into several smaller working sessions.

_____27_____

SETTING THE CONTEXT

When you gather teammates together to work these exercises, you will do yourself a favor by setting the proper context for this "working session." Discussing these topics is not a random or ad hoc activity. The strategic nature of these discussions needs to be set firmly in a proper marketing process so everyone will understand the resulting marketing plan and, more importantly, how to consistently apply the positioning and messaging in everything from corporate presentations to sales tools to social media.

Definition and architecture of an integrated marketing campaign can be reviewed in my book, *Marketing Campaign Development: What marketing executives need to know about architecting global integrated marketing campaigns* (available on Amazon.com). In that book, I introduce the campaign development process as having three phases: kickoff, synchronization, and decision. The persona, positioning statement, and message box templates are key ingredients that fuel the "kickoff" phase. Marketers under pressure execute tactics in a "Ready, Fire! Fire! Fire!" frenzy. The campaign development process reinforces the importance of taking a small amount of time to "Aim." And, the kickoff phase is all about aiming. Rather than having the team guess at the strategy, the kickoff phase is about providing your marketing community of employees, contractors, and consultants with a clear, documented direction of the marketing segmentation and messaging strategies that will, in turn, drive their selection of marketing tactics. Now we're back to *"Ready, Aim, Fire!"*

If you already have a defined marketing process, you can reinforce how and where these exercises fit. If you don't yet have a defined operational process, all you need to do is take a few minutes to say that this information will be collected and summarized in a short document that will become the high-level campaign creative brief—a reference document that will guide the prioritization of marketing tactics. And with that, you're ready to dig in.

_____28_____

SEGMENTATION PRIORITIZATION VIA THE BULL'S EYE EXERCISE

Prioritizing segments is often a challenge, because sales and marketing representatives may have different perspectives. This is precisely why marketers need to wrestle this topic to the ground. If marketing and sales aren't locked in alignment in the planning stage, there is little hope they will be aligned when lead-generation activities start. What happens next is the old argument of sales complaining that marketing is producing no leads, while marketing is wondering what sales did with all the leads they gave them. Chances are that the failure to identify and prioritize market segments is the culprit. As a rule of thumb, I always ask a senior sales leader (typically a VP) to participate in this exercise. I ask her to describe to the team the types of leads she wants in the next six months: who, in what industry, in what size company, with what characteristics? Notice that I have framed the question with a time period: six months. I don't know about you, but my crystal ball is somewhat hazy, especially when I am asked to focus beyond six months.

I recommend approaching the exercise in a "first things first" approach. Where is the easiest market to win? What marketing "beachhead" must we win in order to gain competitive advantage? What types of deals are we most at risk of losing? All of these questions help frame the prioritization of segments. The challenge here is to balance sales' need to win deals this quarter with the longer-term equity that comes from building a consistent and continuous market presence. We need to do both.

Place flip charts around the room and describe a possible target segment on each one. Follow the bull's eye technique described earlier to articulate the *who, where, and why* questions. If you find that multiple segments share relevant characteristics or pain points, go ahead and combine them. Then ask the team to prioritize these segments. If we could only tackle one segment in the next six months, which should it be? Each team member gets one vote. The outcome is the recommended prioritization.

_____29_____

TIPS FOR LEADING THE PERSONA EXERCISE

Once the bull's eye has been identified, we next turn our attention to illustrating a persona who resides in the segment. I often ask a sales rep to tell me about a sale they just won. Assuming that the company would enjoy more wins of a similar nature, this is a good way to start the exercise. Again, I will have flip charts placed around the room. As the sales rep talks about his recent win, I listen for demographic and psychographic details and note them on the flip charts. If this fails to produce a clear picture, I guide the team to produce a persona hypothesis. I ask them, "What feels right?" Even if you don't have a load of market research to fall back on, I will lay odds that the team's gut instincts will be close to reality. (Of course, you won't know that until you socialize and test the hypothesis with others not in the room, especially some friendly customers. See Chapter 35 for next steps for socializing the output.)

This is the beginning of a creative brainstorming activity that can last all day if you aren't careful. Instead, pay attention to team dynamics and let the discussion evolve for thirty minutes. For quicker results, distribute a blank persona template to team members prior to the meeting. Ask them to come prepared with an illustration of who they believe the target persona should be. Ask participants to share their illustrations, comparing and contrasting the different options. If this topic is part of a larger agenda, a break will follow. I use the break time (about fifteen minutes) to quickly decipher the input noted on the flipcharts and build my own persona based on the team's inputs. When the team returns, I ask them to review the collective hypothesis and help me refine it. By the end of the session, the team will have created a persona that feels real and represents an ideal target in the bull's eye segment.

A persona-development case study

When I work with teams, everyone is always politically conscious of the surroundings. While this is a respectful trait, it can lead to some self-editing that can hurt the exercise. A case in point: I was working with a technology company that sells test equipment to laboratories. At the beginning of the workshop, the team seemed convinced there was just one persona—the lab manager. The group sat quietly, agreeing with everything, so as to not be argumentative or cause conflict. I wondered if the market could really be so one-dimensional.

I broke the team into two smaller groups and asked each to work the exercise. Twenty minutes into the exercise, one group started to laugh. I came over to find out what was so funny. Silence followed, only to broken by an escaping giggle. With some embarrassment they introduced me to their persona, Steve: "He's a slacker."

"What do you mean?" I asked.

"Well, he's slightly overweight and not a very outgoing person." Nods of agreement. More laughter.

"Go on," I encouraged.

"Look, he's been in his job for at least fifteen years," someone else offered. "He's become complacent and isn't interested in making waves or even being seen at work. He does the bare minimum to get by." I could feel intensity and animosity building for this persona.

"It's tough selling to these guys because they just don't want to talk to us, even though we know we could help them do so much. These guys are slackers," she concluded with a roll of her eyes.

The other group, overhearing this description, became adamant. "Steve is not the right persona; it's Dr. K. Dr. K is a 'thinker'. He works hard to make his mark and then moves up in the organization." This was when the "Aha!" moment materialized.

Laughing at the derogatory portrait of the "slacker" had me asking why that term was applicable. That led to a broader debate about the personae. As the two teams compared and contrasted their notes, it became clear to everyone that there were indeed two very different personae, each with plenty of examples. At the conclusion of the exercise two personae emerged with two very different stories. Soon after, two different message boxes were created and used in two related, but different, lead-generation programs.

_____30_____

TIPS FOR LEADING THE POSITIONING STATEMENT EXERCISE

Running a successful positioning statement exercise requires the team do some pre-work. With this in mind, it is helpful to address the positioning statement a day or a week *after* the bull's eye and persona exercises have been completed. There are two reasons for this. First, because the first line in the fill-in-the-blank positioning statement exercise is the targeted persona. You will want the team to be very familiar with this persona before tackling the positioning statement. Second, ask all participants to take fifteen minutes to sketch a positioning statement based on their own insights and perspectives about the persona and the product. Ideally, ask them to email you their versions twenty-four to forty-eight hours before the meeting. You'll immediately see if the team shares a common alignment, or if perceptions vary wildly. For obvious reasons, it is very helpful to know this before diving into the positioning statement exercise.

The agenda for the exercise is simple: take each line item one by one. The target persona will have already been completed, so the first major debate will be on the product name and category lines, then the benefit line, and finally the differentiator line. In true brainstorming fashion, the moderator should capture all input on a white board or flip chart. Do not judge the output yet. Wait for the team to respond. Remember, the positioning statement is *not* the message to the customer. Your first draft will be wordy, clunky, and not grammatically correct. I don't care, and neither should you. You want to sketch your first draft quickly so you can spend the rest of the time refining it. After all, it is easier to edit than to create. Plan on having at least two hours for a meaty discussion about your positioning statement. If you complete your draft early, double check it based on the criteria checklist. Chances are you've made some gross assumptions or taken shortcuts that will deflate the power of your positioning statement. As was the case with the persona exercise, the output will need to be socialized and tested with a larger group. Allow time for this to happen; regroup the team in a week or so to refine the draft. It is critical to get the positioning statement right because it will drive everything in the go-to-market strategy, beginning with the message box.

Coaching for the positioning statement facilitator

Occasionally, marketers can feel a bit intimidated by the positioning statement exercise, fearing that colleagues will expect them to already know the answer. While there is no question that marketers who deeply understand the product, technology, and industry are highly valuable, sometimes it is not enough. Familiarity can lead to complacency and acceptance of the status quo. It never hurts to take a fresh perspective and challenge the assumptions. As such, marketers add considerable value by knowing what questions to ask, whether or not they think they know the answers.

Some examples of good probing questions are these:

- *Why did we build this? Why are we offering this product or service?*
- *What's the persona's perception of us?*
- *How have they coped without our solution?*

- *What does the competition offer? How do they position themselves? How are they perceived?*
- *What do we believe are the competition's weaknesses relative to our product or service?*
- *What are the persona's "hot buttons?"*
- *What are the most significant trends affecting our persona and his or her business?*
- *What do we really bring to the table? What's our claim to fame, and why should the persona care?*

31

TIPS FOR LEADING THE MESSAGE BOX EXERCISE

When teams try to tackle the message box first, without the benefit of defining the persona and positioning statement, they waste time and become frustrated in the process. In retrospect, teams that went through the other exercises first were able to complete a draft of their message box in forty-five minutes. To be fair, this was accomplished with the aid of an expert facilitator familiar with the exercise. You will want to have more time, especially the first time you run the exercise.

In practical terms, I have found that small groups of three or four people generate more lively discussions than larger teams. It's too easy to hide in a larger group. Smaller teams invite everyone to participate equally. If you have a team of six or more, break them into smaller groups. One would assume that small groups would come up with similar message boxes; however, this is not always the case. Sometimes, someone will have an "Aha!" moment that will invigorate the creativity in the room. Allow for this to happen. Give each small group a flip chart and forty-five minutes and see what they create.

The most challenging part of this exercise is getting the engagement message correct. Watch out for teams who want to jump to the reinforcement message, claiming it is really an engagement message. (This is very common.) Have each team present their draft and then have the larger group critique them. What do they like? What don't they like?

Coaching for the message box facilitator

Working the magic of the message box takes time and practice. The more you work it, the better and more confident you'll become. Here are six tips to speed you on your way.

1. It's a team sport

The message box should not be developed in isolation. It's meant to be a team exercise. Invite representatives from sales, customer support, and marketing to participate. Each of these groups has a unique perspective of the customer. After a draft is developed, it should be socialized throughout the organization.

2. Ask a sales rep

When teams are not sure where to start, ask a sales rep to walk through a recent sale. How did she engage the prospect? What were they concerned about? How did this conversation unfold? Why did we win this sale? These data points will help you ground the message in reality.

3. Focus on the engagement message first

The hardest thing about the message box is getting the engagement message correct. Once the engagement message is clear and concise, the other messages will almost write themselves. If the engagement message is wrong, then none of the following messages will make any sense. In the course of a forty-five-minute exercise, a team may spend thirty minutes debating the engagement message, and then only need fifteen minutes to draft the solution, reinforcement, and value messages.

4. Use flip charts

Flip charts work better than taking notes on a computer. Place flip charts around the room, where it's easy for everyone to see and contribute. And when conducting a brainstorming session, capture all the ideas without any self-editing or judging.

5. Don't confuse the reinforcement and engagement messages

When product information bubbles up in the engagement message, it's a sign that the team has actually jumped to the reinforcement message. All is not lost. This is natural because the team is most familiar with the product. But it represents a problem area. The facilitator needs to be alert to catch this and properly redirect the team back to the problem the persona is trying to solve.

6. Don't forget to test the messaging

Once a working draft is developed, you are not done. The draft needs to be tested. The best way to know if your story works is to try it on real prospects. Reach out to friendly customers and run it by them. Get their feedback. Have the sales reps start using the message box as an elevator pitch. See how it works.

32

WHO SHOULD LEAD THESE EXERCISES?

Larger companies may have an "integrated campaign manager," a "launch boss," or a "marketing operations manager" who might lead these exercises. Regardless, everyone in the marketing organization will benefit from knowing these best practices and participating in their development.

If your organization doesn't have a central role to guide these discussions, they can actually be led by anyone. Press relations (PR) managers are typically first to execute against a marketing strategy. This was true when I was the PR manager at HP. I took advantage of that by inviting a cross-functional team to develop a positioning statement that would not only benefit me and the press release I was working on, but it also benefited the marketers working on the ads, events, and direct mail pieces that would soon follow. In the same manner, a direct marketer or an advertiser can lead these exercises. It doesn't really matter, as long as it gets done.

For marketers looking to grow their career, jumping in and taking the lead to moderate these discussions is an excellent way to get visibility with the broader team and leadership staff. If you aren't sure, bring up the topic during a staff meeting. Ask a few peers what they think about either your leading an exercise or asking them to lead one. When people understand that the point of these exercises is not to make extra work but to help everyone work faster and produce better, more relevant messages and materials, the value becomes obvious.

33

TIPS FOR GUIDING LARGER TEAMS

Managing cross-functional team dynamics can be a challenge. Here are a few pointers to keep these exercises on track.

1) Keep the core group small

These exercises are best conducted within a small group of four to eight people. Larger groups bring dynamics that can be more difficult to control. With that in mind, be selective whom you invite. Each participant should represent a key function and have immediate value to share. Be sure to have at least one sales leader on the team; this will help build marketing and sales alignment. Outside of the core group, arrange for a set of reviewers and advisors that can be consulted individually during the socialization phase of the process.

2) Be respectful

Because you are leading the exercise does not mean that your opinion is more important than anyone else's. Your role is not to be a judge or a dictator. Be respectful of the leadership and capabilities of everyone on the team. People don't like being viewed as "tactical." Everyone has a strategic nature to the function they provide. Avoid the trap of having people perceive your efforts as "lordly" with you looking at them as "serfs" who tend the crops.

3) Moderate the process, but don't dictate the direction

You control the agenda, the ground rules, and the engagement process. But you don't dictate the output. However, as the moderator, you may also want to assume the role of producing the documents that come from the exercises. In so doing, you have control of deciphering the data in a way you think makes the most sense. This is completely appropriate, giving you a chance to edit and refine the materials.

4) Watch your body language

Chances are that if you are leading these exercises you will be more grounded in how they work. Sometimes, input from novice participants can be off-target and even comical. Avoid becoming visibly frustrated or annoyed. Be careful not to exude a condescending attitude. Whatever you do, don't laugh or put them on the defensive. If you do, everyone will stop participating. Word of your insensitivity will spread like wildfire, and you won't be able to regroup the team. Instead, listen to what they have to say and redirect them by asking follow-up questions that will get the group back on track.

5) Don't rush to judgment

As the team facilitator, your first job is to understand the points of view offered by team members. Ask questions to find out where they are coming from.

6) Involve everyone

When you see an obvious weakness in a persona, positioning statement, or message box, you may not want to express the obvious concern yourself. Ask other teammates for their thoughts as they evaluate the drafts. Even though you'll be tempted to rush to judgment, it is often more effective if a teammate comes to the conclusion first. Allowing time for them to contribute to the discussion is a good way to build stronger bonds with the team.

7) Hire a facilitator

If you are not sure where to start, hire a seasoned expert to facilitate a series of these exercises for one of your product lines. Use the "train the trainer" approach to learning how to you can apply these best practices in future meetings.

8) Have an "open door" policy

Make yourself available to team members outside of these exercises. Always be the coach and sounding board. Invite participants to share ideas with you before, during, and after the "working sessions."

_____34_____

TIPS FOR WORKING WITH
START-UPS

The good news about working with teams in smaller companies is that the politics are usually much less of an issue. The downside is that the burden of each exercise rests squarely on your shoulders. Here are a few suggestions for working through the exercises:

1) Partner with the sales leader

Avoid the temptation to develop the marketing strategy by yourself. Involve the VP of sales and perhaps a customer-support rep. Build a team of three. This will help guide your thinking and give you a sounding board to keep you on track.

2) Take initiative

Interview stakeholders individually and then produce a first-draft persona, positioning statement, and message box yourself. However, make it clear that, while you've taken the lead to document it, the team must support the resulting strategy. This is an excellent way to jumpstart the process.

3) Get comfortable with your discomfort

If your company is small and new to market, you may not have wins to look back on. You will need to build a hypothesis of the target buyer and his or her priorities and interests. This can be uncomfortable. Don't let it distract you. Build the best hypothesis you can and then give it to the sales team and have them leverage it in their daily sales activities. They will be in the best position to give you feedback as to whether the persona and messaging are close enough or off the mark.

4) Be confident in your approach

If you are in charge of marketing at a start up you will be called upon to share your marketing plan with the board of directors. Do not make the mistake of appearing uncertain. Be bold in communicating the plan, even if you've made assumptions. Despite the heavy egos found in board members, they will not know your markets as well as you do. Show them the bull's eye slide. Provide a summary of your target personae focused on their job responsibilities, industry segment, and priorities. And provide them with a copy of the positioning statement that will guide everything from your messaging to your go-to-market plan. These three core slides are the foundation of a marketing leader who understands his market with his feet planted firmly in the marketing high ground.

5) Ask for help

If you are not sure how to drive these exercises, hire a seasoned expert to guide you through the process. That way, you'll get real work done and learn how to apply the techniques yourself next time around.

35

SOCIALIZING THE OUTPUT

Congratulations! You've done the research, guided the best practice exercises, and developed a solid marketing plan as a result. But the game is not over. As a marketer who's reached the high ground, your job is just beginning. The insights, perspectives, and lessons learned from the high ground must be shared broadly. Not until every employee has heard (multiple times) and embraced the plan can you rest. In fact, socializing the output and evangelizing the persona, positioning statement, and messaging framework is a large part of the job description of the able-minded marketer. This is nothing short of an on-going, ebb-and-flow dialog that must take place across the company. The tricky part for the marketer is to know the difference between being the customer's advocate and the shepherd of these best practices, as opposed to being the micro-managing dictator of the process and the output.

It is not enough for the marketing team to sit alone on a bench atop the marketing high ground. Everyone must be invited. Development of the go-to-market plan is a team sport. A single person, in isolation from sales, engineering, or customer support should not develop the marketing plan. Ask sales reps to participate in creating or reviewing the persona and the message box. They are the closest to the customer, and so they will have some good perspective to share. Regarding the positioning statement, solicit input from product managers, engineers, and customer-support representatives. Product marketing or product management departments customarily own the positioning statement, but gathering input and feedback from others outside of the core team helps to refine the language.

By now, you will have noticed that I like using flip charts and encouraging team participation in these exercises. The marketing plan will fail to come to life if people don't feel that they were part of the process. This is very true for bigger, distributed marketing teams. Allow time for them to participate, especially if they are remote in European or Asia Pacific offices.

Be a leader of the process and allow time for others to comment. And be flexible, willing to edit and amend the plan, based on comments you receive. But don't feel that you must accept every edit or opinion. Ultimately, after hearing various points of view, the author of the tools (persona, positioning statement, or message box) gets to decide what words to use. As the steward of these best practices, that is your role and that is your right.

Here are a few tactical ideas to help you socialize the output and invite colleagues to join you on the marketing high ground.

- *Develop a core set of slides to broadly share the marketing strategy. Only the marketing team needs the full details of the plan. For everyone else, make a shorter deck using a few key slides: the primary marketing objective, the persona, the positioning statement, and the message box. Consider the tight alignment that would be achieved if everyone in the organization posted those few slides on their office walls.*
- *Be a guest speaker. Just because you draft a few slides and email them doesn't mean that anyone has read them or understood the implications. You*

need to engage the organization by making the plan visible. Getting out in front of groups to talk about the plan and answer their questions about the market is critically important. It's what marketers can do better than any other function. Make the rounds to key staff meetings, starting with regional sales offices, product management, engineering, and customer-support teams. No other outreach effort on your part will work as well to establish your credibility with internal audiences. Not only is this extremely valuable to bringing your marketing plans and programs to life, it is a powerful skill set to hone for your personal career growth.

- **Facilitate a marketing-sales summit twice a year.** *Being the high ground ambassador is very effective as a tool to disseminate information. However, to pursue effective cross-organizational alignment, a different tactic is needed. Carefully structured summits are "working meetings" attended by marketing and sales leaders. They are the perfect venue for sharing plans, gathering feedback, and solidifying a shared understanding of sales' expectations and marketing's goals and objectives.*

Socializing the output is part shepherding the organization to the marketing high ground and part evangelizing the customers' perspective against the market landscape. It is also politically charged. Finesse is required. I cover this topic at length in my book, *Marketing Campaign Development: what marketing executives need to know about architecting global integrated marketing campaigns* (available on Amazon.com). In that book, I provide tactical insight on how to structure meetings to synchronize input from cross-functional team members and socialize output across the company. I also dedicate a chapter to defining and explaining the role of the integrated campaign manager, a usual leader who guides the path to the marketing high ground.

_____36_____

DALE CARNEGIE'S LESSONS ON LEADERSHIP

In my career, I've found that there are many people who are product experts and technology gurus. It was never my personal goal to learn the nuances of products or technologies better than these people. They would always be savvier than I in those areas. And, to be honest, the company didn't need an extra technologist. Instead, I found that my value-add could be in helping the team better understand the market they were serving. To do that, I needed to learn how to work with a diverse set of individuals of varying backgrounds and expertise. I also needed to learn how to guide people who did not report to me. Equally important was in knowing how to manage my boss. In my final analysis, the skills that helped me the most were not technical skills, but leadership skills.

Somewhere along my path to the marketing high ground someone introduced me to Dale Carnegie's book, *How to Win Friends and Influence People*. Of particular interest is a table at the end that summarizes his leadership principles. I've included it here in Table 8. I can attest that these simple principles can make a world of difference. Be mindful of them as you work the exercises with your team. I've been referencing his book for years. It's helped me grow in my career from a line worker to a manager to executive to consultant.

BE A LEADER

A leader's job often includes changing your people's attitudes and behavior. Some suggestions to accomplish this:

Principle 1: Begin with praise and honest appreciation.

Principle 2: Call attention to people's mistakes indirectly.

Principle 3: Talk about your own mistakes before criticizing the other person.

Principle 4: Ask questions instead of giving direct orders.

Principle 5: Let the other person save face.

Principle 6: Praise the slightest improvement and praise every improvement. Be "hearty in your approbation and lavish in your praise."

Principle 7: Give the other person a fine reputation to live up to.

Principle 8: Use encouragement. Make the fault seem easy to correct.

Principle 9: Make the other person happy about doing the things you suggest.

Table 8: Dale Carnegie's principles of leadership[25]

Afterword

The journey to the marketing high ground is not accomplished overnight. In fact, the marketing process never ends. The marketers who continue to be leaders in their fields are the ones who remain ever vigilant in keeping an eye on the customer and their shifting priorities and interests, as well as the broader market landscape. You will find many marketing teams reviewing their personae, positioning statements, and messaging elements at least once a year, often during the annual planning period.

Never forget why these best practices are required. We live in an over-communicated society that has become jaded by marketing hype. The only way our messages will be heard is if we can become relevant to our intended audience. Only then can we hope to make a connection that will improve the return on our marketing investment. A product roadmap and integrated marketing communications program based on clear personae, strong positioning statements, and focused messaging is the only way to cut through the clutter and sustain competitive leadership.

Taken as a whole, the bull's eye, persona, positioning statement, and message box exercises are all about making sacrifices. Intuitively, we know we can't be all things to all people. But making cuts is difficult. Use these best practices to drive the process, prioritize, and do not become emotionally tied to the outcome. While these exercises are simple, they should not be taken lightly. For marketing success, they are not optional. More important than knowledge is having the right attitude. Specifically, this requires an unending thirst for understanding the target audience and how your product can be of service to them. This is how you will reach the marketing high ground.

For more on these best practices, I invite you to visit my blog (http://marketinghighground.wordpress.com). You'll find other tips, tools, and techniques to help you in your journey. Let me know how you've been able to apply these best practices. I'd enjoy hearing of your progress.

Good luck, and good marketing!

Resources

Dog-eared books in my marketing library

Ries, Al and Jack Trout. *The 22 Immutable Laws of Marketing* (An exploration of the laws that govern marketing and human perception). Harper Business, New York, 1993.

Lowell, Laura. *42 Rules of Marketing* (Simple advice for marketers everywhere). Superstar Press, Cupertino, California, 2007.

Kawasaki, Guy. *The Art of the Start* (Marketing best-practices, the Silicon Valley way). Penguin Books, New York, New York, 2004.

Moore, Geoffrey. *Crossing the Chasm* (The marketing game plan for high-tech companies). Harper Business Books, New York, 1991, 2002.

Woods, Steven. *Digital Body Language* (An exploration of how and why B2B marketers must decode their buyers' digital body language to understand the roles, information needs, timing, and buying intentions of their largely faceless and elusive target market). New Year Publishing, LLC, Danville, California, 2009.

Levinson, Jay Conrad. *Guerrilla Marketing* (Secrets for making big profits from your small businesses). Houghton Mifflin Company, New York, 1993.

Levinson, Jay Conrad. *Guerrilla Marketing Online* (The entrepreneur's guide to earning profits on the Internet). Houghton Mifflin Company, New York, 1995.

Carnegie, Dale. *How to Win Friends & Influence People* (A practical guide on how to work with people and improve your team skills). Pocket Books, New York, New York, 1936, revised 1981.

Schultz, Don, Stanley Tannenbaum, and Robert Lauterborn. *Integrated Marketing Communications* (A look at the history of marketing, the concept of integrated marketing, and an illustrated process of how and why it works). NTC Business Books, Chicago, 1993.

Moore, Geoffrey. *Living on the Fault Line* (Secrets to managing companies successfully in light of rapid, discontinuous, disruptive, and technological change). Harper Collins Books, New York, 2002.

Gospe, Mike. *Marketing Campaign Development: What Marketing Executives Need to Know about Architecting Global Integrated Marketing Campaigns* (A practical prescription for B2B marketing leaders trying to determine the optimum marketing communications mix while navigating internal politics). Happy About Inc., Cupertino, California, 2008.

Ries, Al, Jack Trout. *Positioning: The Battle for Your Mind* (Simply the best book on product positioning I've ever read). Warner Books, New York, 1986.

Simmons, Annette. *The Story Factor* (How to use storytelling as the modus operandi for business success). Basic Books, Cambridge, Massachusetts, 2002.

Author

J. Michael (Mike) Gospe, Jr., is an accomplished leader, marketing strategist, and corporate executive who understands what it takes to market and sell to today's business-to-business companies. With more than twenty-five years of experience, his expertise is in integrated marketing and voice-of-the-customer programs, including designing and facilitating Customer Advisory Board (CAB) meetings and executive planning sessions. Mike leads KickStart Alliance's marketing operations practice where, among other things, he conducts team-based "practical application working sessions" to improve the effectiveness of lead generation campaigns and product launches. His fun, practical approach and roll-up-his-sleeves attitude energizes teams, helping them get "real work done," while guiding them to the next level of excellence.

Mike is also a member of San Francisco State University's faculty and teaches the course, *Essentials of Integrated Marketing*. He's authored a number of marketing- and sales-related articles, and is a frequent guest speaker at companies, marketing associations, and university business schools. His first book, *Marketing Campaign Development: what executives need to know about architecting global integrated marketing campaigns* (2008), is available on Amazon.com.

Join me on LinkedIn: www.linkedin.com/in/mikegospe
Follow me on Twitter: www.twitter.com/mikegospe

Other Works

Other works by J. Michael (Mike) Gospe, Jr., include *Marketing Campaign Development: what executives need to know about architecting global integrated marketing campaigns* (2008), available on Amazon.com.

The two most fundamental questions marketers face are:

1. How do I determine the optimum marketing communications mix?

2. How do I best manage internal politics to launch my marketing campaign and nurture it for best results?

Written for marketing leaders at every level, this book is the only practical, pragmatic "how to" guide designed to answer these two key questions.

This unique playbook takes you step-by-step through the disciplined, yet practical, process of designing truly integrated marketing communications plans that work. In it, you'll find a prescription for building a successful, repeatable campaign-development process, including the necessary templates and helpful, practical tips and techniques required for success. The process and best practices revealed in this book have been used at Aspect, HP, Informatica, Sun, Symantec, and many other companies, large and small. You will learn the secrets for optimizing your marketing efforts and achieving an even greater return on your marketing investment.

You can also find more marketing best-practices information, tips, templates, and techniques at: http://marketingcampaigndevelopment.wordpress.com

Notes

1. http://marketingpassionmarketing.blogspot.com/2009/05/philip-kotler-said-marketing-tasks-day.html

2. *The Marketing High Ground© term and concept is used here through the permission of Brian Gentile and the VSP Group.*

3. One of Professor Markle's sayings often used to encourage his students to engage during class.

4. Sun Microsystems, Inc. *1998 Annual Report*, pages 2, 8. "That's why so much of our effort this year has been directed toward what we call the WebTone."

5. Mike Gospe, *Marketing Campaign Development*: what marketing executives need to know about architecting global integrated marketing campaigns, pages 3 – 8, Happy About, 2008 ©.

6. http://thinkexist.com/quotation/great_communicators_have_an_appreciation_for/151503.html

7. This template is a variation of a positioning statement model taught by Nancy Salz of Salz Consulting. Nancy coached marketers at HP who in turn introduced me to this concept circa 1989. I continue to evolve this tool to meet the needs of my business clients.

8. James C. Anderson, James A. Narus, and Wouter van Rossum, *Customer Value Propositions in Business Markets, Harvard Business Review, March 2006.* (Note: whereas value propositions are broad in nature, capturing the cost-benefit relationship that can be applied across all pertinent market segments, the positioning statement is a subset used for marketing communications purposes. Nevertheless, the three value proposition types offered by the authors apply equally to positioning statements.)

9. "The Globetrotter" persona was developed with Ted Ray for his company FlyRight (www.jetlagformula.com). Reference to this persona is used with permission.

10. "The Conflicted Procrastinator" persona was developed with the LiveOps (www.liveops.com) marketing team led by Paul Lang. Reference to this persona is used with permission.

11. "The Corporate Radical" persona was developed with the Overtone (www.overtone.com) marketing team led by Craig Brennan. Reference to this persona is used with permission.

12. Jack Trout and Al Ries are experts in positioning. See their books *Positioning, the Battle for Your Mind,* Warner Books, New York, 1986, and *The 22 Immutable Laws of Marketing*, Harper Business Press, New York, 1993.

13. This RCA advertising ran in the November 1992 issue of *Sunset Magazine*, page 121.

14. The table of Common Evidence Mistakes was developed by Susan Thomas and Tobey Fitch. It is referenced here with permission.

15. Guy Kawasaki, *The Art of the Start,* Penguin Books, 2004, London, pg 40-41

16. Annette Simmons, *The Story Factor*, Basic Books, NY, 2002, pg 3

17. Note: "But what about the channel?" I hear you ask. The channel sales model adds an additional layer of complexity because, not only do we need to market to the channel partners (to encourage them to do business with us), we must also help them deliver the message to the customer. While the channel-customer process will share similarities to the direct-sales process, there are some important differences. On top of that, the manufacturer-channel-engagement process requires careful attention to minimize channel conflict and optimize sales success. Channel-engagement

processes are not covered in this book. For now, I've attempted to simplify this discussion by focusing only on the direct sales angle.

18. The message box technique described here is based on the concept developed by Susan Thomas and Tobey Fitch. It is referenced with their permission.

19. FlyRight's message-box story for the frequent flyer business executive. It is used here with permission. (www.Jetlagformula.com)

20. This message box was developed in conjunction with Paul Lang, then a VP of product management with a major call-center-platform company. This story sparked creative discussion amongst the global product management team, as they crafted product-use cases. It is used here with permission.

21. Charlene Li and Josh Bernoff, *Groundswell*, Harvard Business Press, 2008 Forrester Research, In. inside book jacket.

22. Overtone's message box, used with permission. (www.overtone.com)

23. This wonderful list of message killers comes from the marketing vault of Susan Thomas and Tobey Fitch. The list is used with permission.

24. http://www.heartquotes.net/teamwork-quotes.html

25. Dale Carnegie, *How to Win Friends & Influence People*, Pocket Books, 1981, pgs 248 – 249.